DK Children's COOKBOOK

DK

LONDON, NEW YORK, MUNICH,
MELBOURNE, AND DELHI

Project Editor Catherine Saunders
Designer Lisa Crowe
Home Economist and Food Stylist Katharine Ibbs
Design Assistants Lynne Moulding and Justin Greenwood
Assistant Home Economists Lisa Harrison, Sarah Tildesley, Fergal Connolly
Consultant Nicola Graimes
Publishing Manager Cynthia O'Neill Collins
Art Director Mark Richards
Category Publisher Alex Kirkham
Production Rochelle Talary
DTP Designer Dean Scholey

First published in Great Britain in 2004 by Dorling Kindersley Limited,
80 Strand, London WC2R 0RL
A Penguin Company

10

Copyright © 2004 Dorling Kindersley Limited

All images © Dorling Kindersley Limited
For further information see: www.dkimages.com

A CIP catalogue record for this book is available from the British Library.

ISBN-13: 978-1-4053-0588-4

Reproduced by Colourscan
Printed and bound at Toppan

Acknowledgements
The publisher would like to thank the photographer's assistant Michael Hart, especially for the endless cups of tea!
A big thank you to all the young chefs who acted as hand models – Latoya Bailey, Hannah Broom, Natika Clarke,
Hannah Leaman, Toby Leaman, Rozina McHugh, Louis Moorcraft, Lily Sansford, Sadie Sansford, Gabriella Soper,
Olivia Sullivan-Davis, James Tilley, and Hope Wadman.

Discover more at
www.dk.com

DK Children's COOKBOOK

Recipes by Katharine Ibbs
Photography by Howard Shooter

Contents

p.12-13

p.42-43

p.70-71

⭐ Desserts

p.86-87

p.72-73

⭐ Tools   120-121

⭐ Glossary   122-125

⭐ Index   126-128

⭐ Baking

p.110-111

p.80-81

Introduction

Whether you want to learn how to cook or are already a budding chef, this is the book for you!

Cooking is great fun and this book introduces you to key cooking techniques – from mashing to marinating and from boiling to baking. And with over 50 tasty recipes to choose from, there is something for everyone!

Having a healthy diet

It is important to take care of your body so that you feel healthy and happy. One of the best ways to do this is to eat a balanced diet. This means that your meals should contain a balance of the main food groups – protein, carbohydrates, fibre, fat, and vitamins and minerals.

★ Protein

This helps you to grow. It also builds up your muscles and helps your body to work properly. Meat, fish, dairy products (such as milk, eggs, and cheese), pulses (such as peas, beans, and lentils), and nuts are good sources of protein.

★ Carbohydrates

These give you energy so that you can grow and lead an active life. Potatoes, cereals (such as wheat, which is used to make bread and pasta), grains (such as rice and oats), and pulses (such as peas, beans, and lentils) are good sources of carbohydrates.

★ Fibre

Your body needs fibre to help keep your intestines healthy and working properly. Cereals (such as wheat in wholemeal bread), pulses (such as peas, beans, and lentils), and fruit and vegetables (especially those with their skin on such as apples and potatoes) all contain fibre.

★ Fat

Although too much of it is bad for you, fat is still an important nutrient. It is a good source of energy and helps your body to absorb some vitamins. The best kinds of fat are polyunsaturated and monounsaturated. Foods that contain these fats are oily fish (such as tuna and salmon), avocados, nuts, seeds and oils (such as olive oil, sunflower oil, and vegetable oil).

★ Vitamins and minerals

Vitamins help your body to work properly and minerals help your body to grow and repair itself, which is important for healthy skin, bones, and teeth. If you eat a healthy diet, you should get all the vitamins and minerals that you need. As well as three well-balanced meals every day, you should eat plenty of fresh fruit and vegetables because they are excellent sources of vitamins and minerals.

How to use the recipes

Every page is packed full of information about cooking techniques, healthy eating, and staying safe in the kitchen. Each recipe has an easy-to-follow design, which is explained below. So relax, have fun, and GET COOKING!

Difficulty ratings help you to pick the most suitable recipes.
1= easy
2 = medium
3 = hard

Estimated preparation and cooking times help you to plan your meals.

A tools checklist helps you to gather everything that you need before you start cooking.

Techniques that appear in the glossary are highlighted in the recipes and at the top of the page.

The ingredients are pictured to help you find them, but remember, they do not show the exact quantities!

This symbol warns you to take extra care because the step involves heat or sharp objects.

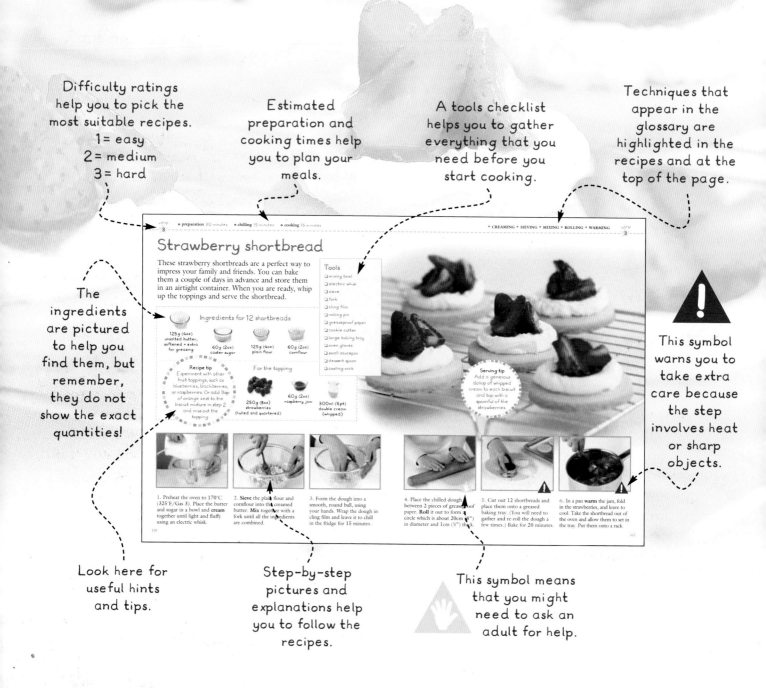

Look here for useful hints and tips.

Step-by-step pictures and explanations help you to follow the recipes.

This symbol means that you might need to ask an adult for help.

Cooking rules

These recipes have been specially created to help you learn both basic cooking skills and more advanced techniques. Follow these simple guidelines for fun, safe, and successful cookery.

★ Golden rules

1. Be safe – always take care when you see this symbol, especially when using sharp knives, or hot hobs and ovens.
2. Be sensible – ask an adult for help and advice if you need it, especially when you see this symbol.
3. Be clean – always wash your hands before you start cooking, tie back long hair, and wear an apron to protect your clothes.
4. Be prepared – always read the recipe thoroughly and gather all the ingredients and tools you need before starting to cook.
5. Be consistent – when following a recipe use either metric or imperial weights and measures, never mix them. All teaspoon and tablespoon measurements refer to level, not heaped, spoonfuls.

★ Hygiene rules

1. Wash all fruit and vegetables before cooking or eating.
2. Always use separate chopping boards for meat and vegetables.
3. Don't spread germs – always wash your hands thoroughly before and after cooking, especially after touching raw meat or fish.
4. Wash up as you go along and make sure that you have a cloth handy to wipe up any spills or mess.
5. Store cooked and raw food separately.
6. Keep meat and fish in the fridge until needed and ensure they are cooked properly.
7. Always check the "best before" and "use-by" dates on all ingredients. Never use out-of-date food.

★ Heat rules

1. Always use oven gloves when handling hot pans, trays, and bowls.
2. Don't put hot things directly onto the work surface. Always use a trivet, mat, or sturdy wooden board.
3. When you are cooking on the hob, turn the pan handles to the side (away from the heat) so that you are less likely to knock them.
4. When you are stirring food on the hob, grip the handle firmly to steady the pan.

★ Chef's rules

1. Be creative – cooking is supposed to be fun, so relax and don't be scared to adapt the recipes to suit your personal tastes.
2. Be confident – cooking is about trying new things. Just go for it and cook up a storm!
3. Be calm – take your time and don't panic if the food doesn't turn out quite how you hoped. Most likely it will still taste great, or you will have learnt a valuable lesson for next time!
4. Vary your meals – don't eat the same thing all the time. A balanced diet also means that you should eat different types of food.

Breakfast

After a good night's sleep, your body will be running low on energy and essential nutrients. Eating a good breakfast will wake you up and make you ready to face the day's challenges. Whether it is a tough day at school, where you need to concentrate, or a fun-filled weekend, where you will be constantly active, it is really important to start your day the right way.

The best foods to eat for breakfast are those that are high in fibre and carbohydrates. Good foods for this are wholemeal bread, cereal, and oats because they all slowly release energy throughout the day. Fresh fruit is also great because it gives you a healthy burst of vitamins to start the day, while an egg-based breakfast will provide you with protein to build and repair your body.

● **preparation** 5–10 minutes ● **cooking** none

Fruit smoothie

Smoothies are easy to make and taste delicious at any time of day. Follow these four simple steps for a burst of fruity goodness.

1. Rinse and drain the strawberries in cold water and then **hull** them by holding the pointed end and slicing off the stem.

Ingredients for 2-4 servings

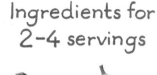

1 ripe banana

200g (7oz) ripe strawberries

200ml (7fl oz) milk

1tbsp of clear runny honey (optional)

100ml (3½fl oz) natural yoghurt

Recipe idea
Replace the banana and strawberries with a large mango and half a medium melon and use 100ml (3½fl oz) orange juice and 1tbsp lime juice instead of milk.

Tools
❑ sharp knife
❑ chopping board
❑ measuring spoons
❑ blender

2. Cut the strawberries in half and put them to one side. Peel the banana and throw away the skin. **Slice** the banana, for easy blending in step 4.

3. Carefully put the banana and strawberries into the blender. Add the milk, yoghurt, and honey and put the lid on securely.

4. Blend the mixture until it is completely smooth. Pour the smoothie into tall glasses and enjoy – what a great way to start the day!

Chef's tip
For an ice-cool summer treat, add a scoop or two of ice cream to the smoothie mixture in step 3.

● **preparation** 5 minutes   ● **cooking** 5-10 minutes

Boiled eggs

Eggs can be cooked in a variety of different ways and are an excellent source of protein. The simplest method is to boil them for a delicious and nutritious breakfast. The most important thing to remember when boiling eggs is timing because this makes the difference between a soft-boiled egg and a hard-boiled egg.

⚠️

1. Half-fill a small saucepan with water and place it on the hob. Gently lower the eggs into the pan and bring the water to the boil.

Ingredients for 2 servings

2 eggs

To serve

2 slices of wholemeal bread

spreadable butter or margarine

Tools
❑ small saucepan
❑ slotted spoon
❑ toaster
❑ bowl of cold water
❑ 2 egg cups
❑ teaspoon

2. **Boil** the eggs for 4 minutes. While the eggs are cooking, you can make the toast. Place the bread in the toaster and toast until golden brown.

3. Remove the eggs with a slotted spoon and briefly dip them in cold water. This will cool the eggs and prevent them from cooking any further.

4. Place each egg in an egg cup and tap the top with the back of a teaspoon. Carefully slice off the top with the spoon. Serve with strips of buttered toast.

Food fact
Although the yolk of your soft-boiled egg will be runny, a properly-cooked egg should always have a firm egg white. If the white of your egg is still runny, it hasn't been cooked for long enough!

Chef's tip
For hard-boiled eggs, boil the eggs for 6–7 minutes and make sure that they cool completely in step 3.

● preparation 10 minutes ● cooking 15 minutes

Crunchy cereal

This breakfast recipe is definitely worth getting out of bed for! Create a homemade cereal that is full of important fibre and carbohydrates with a tasty combination of oats, fruit, nuts, and seeds.

Tools

- ☐ sharp knife
- ☐ chopping board
- ☐ measuring spoons
- ☐ medium saucepan
- ☐ wooden spoon
- ☐ non-stick baking tray
- ☐ oven gloves
- ☐ plate
- ☐ large mixing bowl

Ingredients for 6 servings

1tbsp of olive oil

3tbsp of golden syrup

175g (6oz) jumbo rolled oats

60g (2oz) Brazil nuts (optional)

Recipe idea
Try other dried fruits, nuts, or seeds. Raisins, tropical fruits, hazelnuts, or pumpkin seeds, would all taste great in this recipe!

30g (1oz) sunflower seeds

60g (2oz) dried pineapple pieces

60g (2oz) dried banana chips

60g (2oz) dried apricots

60g (2oz) toasted coconut flakes (optional)

To serve
one of the following

milk

natural or flavoured yoghurt

1. **Chop** the brazil nuts into medium-sized pieces. Remember, if you are allergic to nuts or do not like them, you can miss out this step.

2. Preheat the oven to 200°C (400°F/Gas 6). Pour the oil and syrup into the saucepan. Gently warm them over a low heat until they melt together.

3. Ensure that the heat has been turned off and then tip the oats, nuts, and sunflower seeds into the melted syrup mixture. Stir until well coated.

This cereal will stay fresh for up to two weeks if you store it an airtight container.

Serving tip
Serve your cereal in a bowl with milk or a dollop of your favourite yoghurt.

4. Tip the oat mixture onto a baking tray. Put it in the preheated oven for 10 minutes, or until the edges turn golden and the oats form clusters.

5. Cut the pineapple pieces in half, quarter the apricots, and break the banana chips into small pieces. **Mix** all the fruit and coconut together in a bowl.

6. Spoon the oat clusters onto a plate and leave them to cool for a few minutes. Add the oat clusters to the bowl of fruit and coconut and mix them together.

● **preparation** 5 minutes ● **cooking** 5 minutes

Scrambled eggs

Get cracking with this great breakfast idea!
The secret of scrambled eggs is not to
overcook them in step 4 otherwise they
will become dry and rubbery.

1. To **crack** the eggs, tap
each one in turn on the side
of the bowl. Then gently pull
the shell apart so that the
insides drop into the bowl.

Ingredients for 1 serving

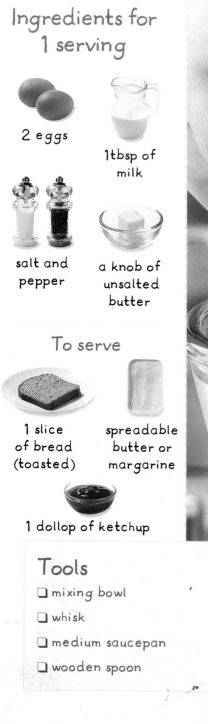

2 eggs

1 tbsp of milk

salt and pepper

a knob of unsalted butter

To serve

1 slice of bread (toasted)

spreadable butter or margarine

1 dollop of ketchup

Tools
- ❏ mixing bowl
- ❏ whisk
- ❏ medium saucepan
- ❏ wooden spoon

See p.125 for expert tips on how to crack an egg like this!

2. Add the milk to the bowl of eggs. Season with salt and black pepper and **whisk** the ingredients together until they are mixed in completely.

3. Over a low heat, gently melt the butter in the saucepan. Take extra care when doing this because if the pan gets too hot, the butter will spit.

4. Carefully pour the beaten egg mixture into the pan and stir constantly for 2–3 minutes. The egg will become a firm scramble but should look moist.

Serving tip
Scrambled eggs taste great on lightly-buttered toast, with a dollop of ketchup!

● **preparation** 10 minutes   ● **cooking** 15 minutes

Breakfast omelette

This omelette is a tasty variation of a traditional breakfast fry-up. It has all the right ingredients for a filling weekend brunch – eggs, bacon, tomato, mushrooms – and could even be served with a green salad as a light or main meal.

Tools

- ❑ whisk
- ❑ jug
- ❑ grater
- ❑ wooden spoon
- ❑ sharp knife
- ❑ 2 chopping boards
- ❑ small non-stick frying pan or omelette pan
- ❑ wooden spatula
- ❑ 2 plates
- ❑ kitchen paper

The omelette should be firm but still moist when it is cooked in step 6.

Recipe idea
Experiment with different fillings, such as ham, onions, courgettes, peppers, or even plain cheese!

Ingredients for 1 omelette

2 eggs

30g (1oz) cheddar cheese

2tbsp of milk

a knob of unsalted butter

salt and pepper

For the filling

2 rashers of bacon

1tsp of sunflower oil

60g (2oz) mushrooms

1 tomato

hard

3

1. **Whisk** the eggs and milk together in a jug. (This will make it easy to pour in step 5.) **Grate** the cheese and stir it in to the egg mixture. Season.

2. Cut the tomato into chunks and **slice** the mushrooms. On a separate board, remove the rind from the bacon and cut the meat into cubes.

3. Place the frying pan over a medium heat and **fry** the bacon for 3 minutes or until cooked completely. Tip the bacon onto a plate, lined with kitchen paper.

4. Heat the oil and fry the mushrooms for 2 minutes. Add the tomato to the pan and cook for 1 minute. Put the tomato and mushrooms onto a plate.

5. Melt the butter in the pan. Pour in the egg so that it covers the base of the pan. Cook the egg on a medium heat until the edges begin to cook and set.

6. Using a spatula, push the cooked egg into the centre of the pan. The uncooked egg will run to the sides. Repeat until all the egg is cooked.

7. Shake the pan to release the omelette and spoon the filling over one half. Slide the omelette out onto a plate and gently flip the unfilled half over the top.

● preparation 15 minutes ● standing 30 minutes (optional) ● cooking 20 minutes

Mini pancakes

Making batter is a useful skill to learn and the small size makes these pancakes perfect for first-time flippers! Here's a handy tip – if you leave the batter to stand for half an hour before adding the fruit and cooking it, it has a much lighter texture.

Tools
- ❑ sieve
- ❑ mixing bowl
- ❑ wooden spoon
- ❑ whisk
- ❑ measuring jug
- ❑ large frying pan
- ❑ serving spoon or ladle
- ❑ dessert spoon
- ❑ metal spatula

Ingredients for 8 pancakes

150g (5oz) plain flour

1tsp of baking powder

3 pinches of salt

150ml (¼pt) milk

1 egg

30g (1oz) caster sugar

125g (4oz) fresh blueberries

30g (1oz) unsalted butter

Recipe idea
The blueberries can be replaced with 1 large banana (chopped) in step 3. You could even try plain pancakes, served with lemon juice and sugar or just some maple syrup.

To serve
(optional)

1 large banana (peeled and sliced)

maple syrup

1. **Sieve** the flour, baking powder, and salt into the mixing bowl. Stir in the sugar with a wooden spoon and leave to one side.

2. **Crack** the egg into a bowl, add it to the milk, and **whisk** them together. It is best to do this in a jug so the mixture can be poured easily in step 3.

3. Pour the milk and egg mixture into the flour and **beat** with a wooden spoon. Gently **fold** in the blueberries, taking care not to crush them.

See p.123–125 for tips on the techniques used in this recipe.

Serving tip
These pancakes taste great served with slices of banana and some maple syrup.

4. Over a medium heat, melt a quarter of the butter in a large frying pan. When the butter begins to bubble, you are ready to start cooking!

5. Ladle two spoonfuls of batter into the frying pan. **Fry** the pancakes for 2 minutes or until bubbles appear on top and the undersides turn golden.

6. Use a metal spatula to **flip** the cakes. Cook the other side for 2 minutes, or until the cakes are cooked through. Repeat with the rest of the batter.

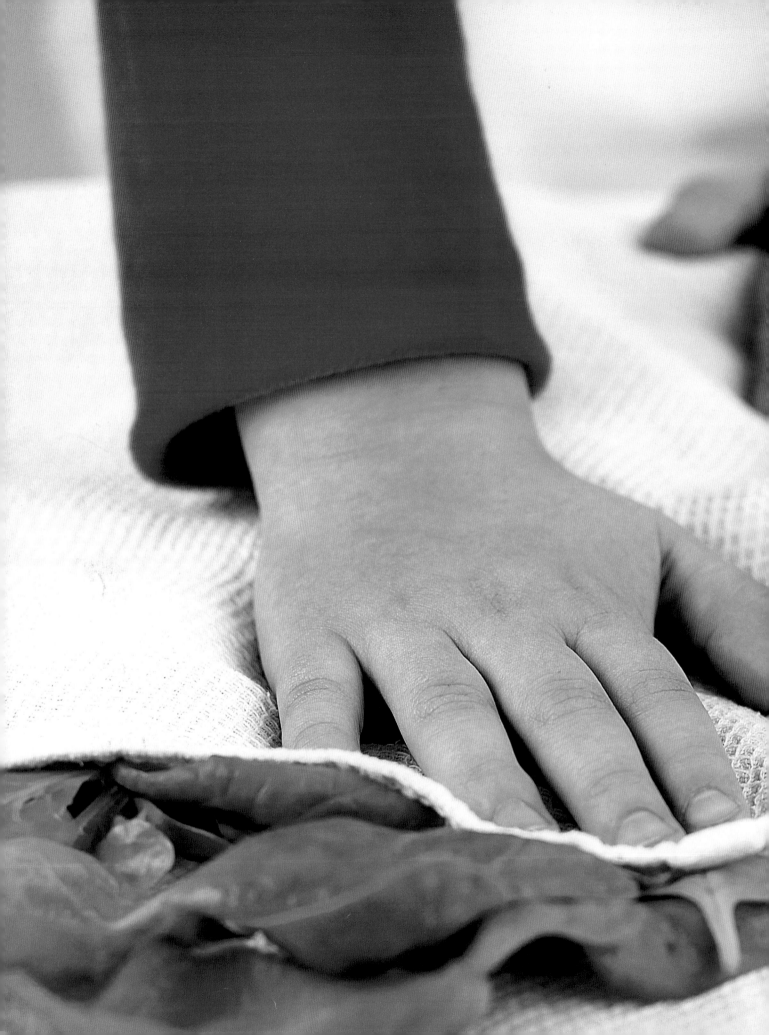

Light meals

This section introduces some great ideas for tasty lunches and light meals. Every meal that you eat should have a healthy balance of essential nutrients. If you are eating in the middle of the day, it is very important to eat the kinds of food that will satisfy your hunger and give you energy but will not make you too full to have any fun in the afternoon!

You will also learn some important new skills and techniques in this section, from slicing and dicing to marinating and grilling. Remember to refer to the glossary on p.122-125 for extra tips!

● preparation 15 minutes ● cooking none

Green salad with dressing

Salad is delicious as a light meal or snack and can also be served as a nutritious accompaniment to a main meal.

1. Spoon all the dressing ingredients into a clean jar and put the lid on tightly. Shake the jar to **mix** the ingredients together.

Ingredients for 4-6 servings

200g (7oz) mixed salad leaves e.g. lettuce, spinach, watercress

½ large cucumber (diced)

12-18 cherry tomatoes (halved)

For the dressing

3tbsp of olive oil

1tbsp of fresh lemon juice

1tsp of whole grain mustard

salt and pepper

1tsp of clear runny honey

Tools
- ❏ teaspoon
- ❏ jar with secure lid
- ❏ colander
- ❏ clean t-towel
- ❏ large mixing bowl

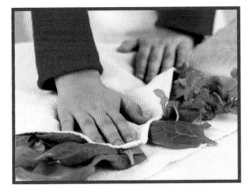

2. Rinse and drain the salad leaves using a colander. Tip them onto a clean t-towel and gently pat dry. Tear the leaves into smaller pieces.

3. Using your hands, carefully mix the salad leaves, cucumber, and tomatoes together in a large bowl. Transfer the mixed salad into individual bowls.

4. Shake the dressing again and **drizzle** some over each bowl of salad. Leave the jar of dressing on the side so that you can add more if you like.

Serving tip
Always drizzle the dressing just before you eat the salad, so that it does not turn soggy!

Try adding other ingredients to your salad such as olives, onions, nuts, cheese, or croûtons (see p.32-33).

Jacket potato

Here's a top tip – if you like the skin of your jacket potato to be firm, roll the potato in a little olive oil after scrubbing it in step 1.

Ingredients for 2 servings

2 large baking potatoes

For the filling

2 tbsp of sour cream

butter (optional)

90g (3oz) broccoli (cut into tiny pieces)

125g (4oz) cheese (grated)

pepper

⚠️

1. Preheat the oven to 200°C (400°F/Gas 6). Scrub the potatoes in cold water, and pat them dry. Prick the potatoes all over with a fork.

Recipe idea
Use your favourite fillings for this recipe – tuna and sweetcorn, baked beans and cheese, or just a little melted butter and a green salad.

Tools
❏ chopping board
❏ fork
❏ roasting tin/baking tray
❏ sharp knife
❏ saucepan
❏ colander
❏ mixing bowl
❏ dessert spoon
❏ kitchen paper

2. **Bake** the potatoes for 1–1½ hours or until they are soft in the centre. Carefully remove the potatoes from the oven and cut a cross in the top of each.

3. While the potatoes are baking, boil the broccoli for 4 minutes. Drain the broccoli and **mix** it with the cheese and sour cream. Season with pepper.

4. Using kitchen paper to protect your hands, squeeze the bottom corners of each potato to open it up. Take care, the potatoes will still be very hot!

When the potato is cooked it will be soft in the middle. Use a knife or skewer to check this.

Serving tip
Spread some butter on your potato and spoon over the filling. The cheese, butter, and sour cream will melt together and taste yummy!

Dips and dippers

These recipes are great as snacks but they can also be served with some of the other recipes. For example, potato wedges taste great with the burgers on p.40–41 and guacamole goes well with the chicken wraps on p.54–55.

Tools

- ❏ kitchen scissors
- ❏ 2 non-stick baking trays
- ❏ oven gloves
- ❏ pastry brush
- ❏ sharp knife
- ❏ chopping board
- ❏ roasting tin
- ❏ food processor
- ❏ dessert spoon
- ❏ mixing bowl

Ingredients for 6-8 servings

potato wedges

4 small baking potatoes

2 tbsp of olive oil

1 tsp of ground paprika

salt and pepper

guacamole

3 ripe avocados

½ red onion (finely diced)

1 garlic clove (crushed)

juice of 1 lime

salt and pepper

2 tomatoes (de-seeded and diced)

2 tbsp of chopped fresh coriander (optional)

3-4 dashes of pepper sauce (optional)

houmous

400g (13oz) can chick peas

3 tbsp of olive oil

½ tsp of ground cumin

2 tbsp of Tahini paste

1 garlic clove (chopped)

juice of ½ lemon

tortilla chips

4 flour tortillas

salt and pepper

30g (1oz) unsalted butter (melted)

Tortilla chips

1. Preheat the oven to 180°C (350°F/Gas 4). Cut the tortillas into quarters and then cut them in half, to make 32 triangles. Lay them on baking trays.

2. Brush each piece with melted butter and season. Bake for 10–12 minutes or until crisp and golden. Allow the tortillas to cool before eating.

Potato wedges

1. Preheat the oven to 220°C (425°F/Gas 7). Scrub each potato, pat dry, and cut them in half lengthways. Cut each half into three equal wedges.

2. **Mix** the oil, paprika, salt, and pepper together in a roasting tin. **Coat** the wedges in the mixture and bake for 40–45 minutes. Shake the pan occasionally.

Chef's tip
Season the houmous with salt and pepper and sprinkle with a little paprika for decoration!

Houmous

1. Drain and then rinse the chick peas. Tip them into the food processor, add the remaining houmous ingredients, and **blend** until smooth.

Guacamole

1. Cut the avocados in half, working around the stone. Scoop out the stone and then the avocado flesh. Finely **chop** the flesh and put it into a bowl.

2. Put the onion, garlic, lime juice, tomato, pepper sauce, and coriander into the mixing bowl. Season and then mix all the ingredients together. Serve.

Tomato soup

Soup is the perfect choice for a light meal or as a starter for a special dinner party. This recipe for thick and tasty tomato soup includes carrots, thyme, and garlic for extra flavour and is topped with cubes of toasted bread, called croûtons.

Tools

- ☐ sharp knife
- ☐ peeler
- ☐ chopping board
- ☐ medium saucepan
- ☐ wooden spatula
- ☐ bread knife
- ☐ non-stick baking tray
- ☐ oven gloves
- ☐ ladle
- ☐ blender

Ingredients for 2-4 servings

- 1 small onion
- 1 small carrot
- 400g (13oz) can chopped tomatoes
- 1tbsp of tomato purée
- 2tbsp of olive oil
- 1 garlic clove, crushed (optional)
- 1tbsp of plain flour
- black pepper
- 1 pinch of granulated sugar
- 1tsp of fresh thyme leaves (optional)
- 450ml (¾pt) vegetable stock
- 1 squeeze of fresh lemon juice

For the croûtons

- 2 thick slices of bread
- 2tbsp of olive oil
- salt and pepper

1. Preheat the oven to 220°C (425°F/Gas 7). **Peel** and **chop** the onion and carrot (see p.122). Heat the oil in the saucepan, over a medium heat.

2. Add the onion and carrot and cook for about 5 minutes to soften, stirring occasionally. Stir in the garlic and flour and cook the mixture for 1 minute.

3. Add the tomatoes, purée, thyme, stock, sugar, and lemon juice to the pan and bring to the boil. Reduce the heat and **simmer** for 20–25 minutes.

If you like your soup less thick, add 600ml (1pt) stock in step 3.

Serving tip
Serve the tomato soup with a scattering of croûtons. Add a dollop of sour cream for extra flavour!

4. Meanwhile, cut the bread into 2cm (¾") cubes. Scatter the bread on to the baking tray and **drizzle** over the olive oil. Season with salt and pepper.

5. Use your hands to **coat** the bread in the oil. Bake for 8–10 minutes, until crisp and golden. Shake the tray every few minutes for even cooking.

6. Carefully ladle the hot soup into the blender. Season the soup with pepper, and **blend** until smooth. Ladle the soup into bowls and serve.

● **preparation** 20 minutes ● **marinating** 30 minutes (optional) ● **cooking** 10 minutes

Marinated chicken

The chicken in this recipe is marinated so that it absorbs the curry flavour. If you don't have time you can miss out the marinating and go straight to cooking in step 3. Alternatively, you could marinate for longer for a more intense flavour.

Tools
- ❏ mixing bowl
- ❏ dessert spoon
- ❏ 2 chopping boards
- ❏ 2 sharp knives
- ❏ frying pan
- ❏ wooden spatula

Ingredients for 2-4 servings

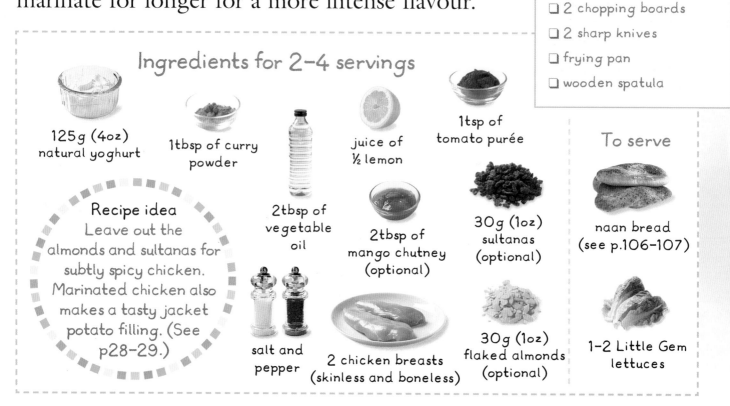

125g (4oz) natural yoghurt

1tbsp of curry powder

2tbsp of vegetable oil

juice of ½ lemon

1tsp of tomato purée

2tbsp of mango chutney (optional)

30g (1oz) sultanas (optional)

30g (1oz) flaked almonds (optional)

Recipe idea
Leave out the almonds and sultanas for subtly spicy chicken. Marinated chicken also makes a tasty jacket potato filling. (See p28-29.)

salt and pepper

2 chicken breasts (skinless and boneless)

To serve

naan bread (see p.106-107)

1-2 Little Gem lettuces

1. In a bowl, **mix** the tomato purée, oil, and curry powder together to make a paste. Add the lemon juice and half the yoghurt to make the marinade.

2. Carefully cut each chicken breast into **cubes** of about 2.5cm (1"). (See p.122 for expert tips on slicing, dicing, and cubing.)

3. Stir the chicken into the marinade, season with salt and pepper, and cover the bowl. Leave the chicken to **marinate** in the fridge for 30 minutes.

See p.123 for tips on how to check when meat is properly cooked.

Serving tip
Serve the yoghurt left over from step 1 as a side dish. The plain yoghurt tastes great with the curry flavour of the chicken. Stir in the mango chutney for a fruity twist.

4. Place the frying pan over a medium to high heat and **fry** the chicken for 3–4 minutes. The chicken will change colour but it will not be cooked yet.

5. Add the sultanas and almonds and cook for 3–4 minutes. Before serving, cut a piece of chicken in half. If there is no trace of pink, it is cooked.

6. To shred the lettuce, roll up the leaves and carefully cut them into thin slices. Serve the chicken with the shredded lettuce and naan bread.

● preparation 20-25 minutes   ● cooking 10-15 minutes

Pesto toasts

This recipe introduces you to griddling, in step 4. A griddle pan has a ridged design which gives the toasted bread a stripy pattern. Griddling is also a low-fat way of cooking meat or fish as the ridges help excess fat to drain away.

Tools

☐ sharp knife
☐ chopping board
☐ food processor
☐ pastry brush
☐ griddle pan or toaster
☐ tongs
☐ table knife
☐ oven gloves
☐ grill rack and foil-lined tray

Ingredients for 4 servings

For the pesto

1 garlic clove

30g (1oz) fresh Parmesan cheese

1tbsp of pine nuts

black pepper

60g (2oz) fresh basil leaves

3tbsp of olive oil

Recipe idea
The remaining pesto will stay fresh for up to a week, if you keep it in an airtight container in the fridge. Try stirring it into some pasta for a deliciously simple main meal.

For the toasts

fresh crusty bread

1tbsp of olive oil

1 pepper (roasted, skinned, and de-seeded)

1 small ball of mozzarella (drained)

1. Roughly **chop** the garlic and Parmesan cheese and put them in the food processor. Add the pine nuts and check that the lid is securely on the processor.

2. **Blend** the garlic, Parmesan, and pine nuts until they look like fine breadcrumbs. Add the basil and oil and blend again to make a smooth mixture. Season.

3. Cut 4 slices of bread, about 2.5 cm (1") thick and brush both sides with the olive oil. Place the griddle pan over a medium-high heat.

You can buy roasted peppers in supermarkets or roast them yourself (see p.123).

Chef's tip
For a super-quick bite, miss out the grilling part in step 6. Pesto toasts don't need to be cooked to taste great!

4. **Griddle** the bread for 2–3 minutes on each side or until toasted. Don't worry, if you don't have a griddle – grill or toast the bread instead.

5. Slice the ball of mozzarella into 4 equal slices. Tear the pepper and mozzarella into smaller pieces. Preheat the grill to a medium heat.

6. Spread each toast with a layer of pesto and add some pepper and mozzarella. **Grill** for 3 minutes or until the cheese has melted. Season and then serve.

Cheese melt with poached egg

Adding a poached egg makes this recipe a tasty variation of cheese on toast. You can use any type of bread or cheese.

1. Preheat the grill to a medium heat. **Mix** the grated cheese, Worcestershire sauce, beaten egg, and seasoning together in a mixing bowl.

Ingredients for 2 servings

2 bread rolls, muffins, or bagels (halved)

2 slices of ham (halved)

salt and pepper

2-3 dashes of Worcestershire sauce (optional)

1 egg (beaten)

150g (5oz) cheese (grated)

2 eggs

Recipe idea
Leave out the egg or ham, if you prefer a plain cheese melt.

Tools

❏ mixing bowl
❏ foil-lined grill tray and rack
❏ 2 teaspoons
❏ oven gloves
❏ medium saucepan
❏ jug
❏ slotted spoon

2. Toast the rolls on both sides. Place a piece of ham on each half and top with the cheese mix. **Grill** for 3 minutes, or until melted and golden.

3. Meanwhile, crack an egg into a jug and gently tip it into a pan half-full of **simmering** water. Simmer for 3 minutes or until the egg white is cooked.

4. Remove the **poached** egg with a slotted spoon and serve on top of two cheese melts. Repeat step 3 with the second egg, season, and serve.

Chef's tip
Line the grill tray with foil and place the rack on top. This makes the grill easy to wash up because any drips or spills will land on the foil, which can be thrown away.

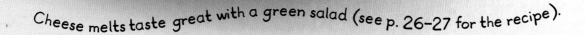

Cheese melts taste great with a green salad (see p. 26–27 for the recipe).

● **preparation** 20–25 minutes ● **chilling** 30 minutes ● **cooking** 15–20 minutes

Hamburgers

This family favourite tastes great when you make it yourself and is lower in fat and higher in taste than shop-bought burgers. See p.66–67 for ideas on how to adapt this recipe to make meatballs.

Tools
- ❏ chopping board
- ❏ sharp knife
- ❏ food processor
- ❏ large mixing bowl
- ❏ wooden spoon
- ❏ large plate
- ❏ cling film
- ❏ oven gloves
- ❏ foil-lined grill tray and rack
- ❏ metal spatula

Ingredients for 6 burgers

500g (1lb) lean minced beef

½ small red onion

2 tbsp of tomato ketchup

1 tsp of mustard (optional)

1 tbsp of Worcestershire sauce (optional)

salt and pepper

1 egg yolk (optional)

1 garlic clove (optional)

For the toppings

2 tomatoes

lettuce leaves

6 cheese slices

6 burger buns

1. Roughly **chop** the onion and garlic. Finely **blend** them and tip them into a bowl. Add the beef, Worcestershire sauce, ketchup, mustard, and egg yolk.

2. Season with salt and pepper and **mix** them all together. It is easiest to start off with a spoon and then use your hands to mix everything together completely.

3. Use your hands to **shape** the mixture into 6 equal-sized balls. Press the top of the balls down to make a flatter burger shape, about 1cm (½") thick.

In summertime these burgers would taste great cooked on a barbecue!

Serving tip
Place the burgers and toppings on a bun, with some ketchup and mayonnaise on the side. Eat with your fingers!

4. Put the burgers onto a plate and cover them with cling film. Chill them for 30 minutes to make the burgers firmer and easier to cook.

5. Preheat the grill to a medium heat. Place the burgers on a grill rack and **grill** them for 6–7 minutes on each side or until thoroughly cooked.

6. While the burgers are cooking, prepare the toppings. Wash the lettuce and tomatoes. Halve the burger buns and then thinly slice the tomatoes.

● **preparation** 15 minutes   ● **cooking** 20 minutes

Pasta salad

Pasta is high in carbohydrates so it is a great source of energy. This recipe also has eggs and tuna for protein, while the beans and tomatoes provide essential vitamins and minerals. Tuna and other oily fish are really good for you and you should try and eat them twice a week.

Tools
- ☐ large saucepan
- ☐ slotted spoon
- ☐ colander
- ☐ sieve
- ☐ plate
- ☐ small saucepan
- ☐ bowl of cold water
- ☐ chopping board
- ☐ sharp knife
- ☐ metal mixing spoon
- ☐ jar with lid
- ☐ large mixing bowl

Ingredients for 4–6 servings

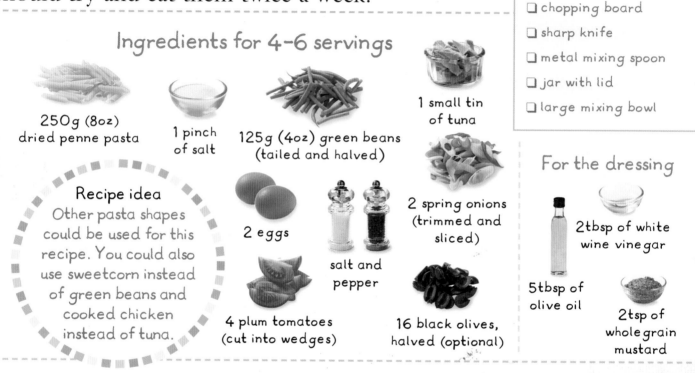

250g (8oz) dried penne pasta

1 pinch of salt

125g (4oz) green beans (tailed and halved)

1 small tin of tuna

Recipe idea
Other pasta shapes could be used for this recipe. You could also use sweetcorn instead of green beans and cooked chicken instead of tuna.

2 eggs

salt and pepper

2 spring onions (trimmed and sliced)

4 plum tomatoes (cut into wedges)

16 black olives, halved (optional)

For the dressing

2tbsp of white wine vinegar

5tbsp of olive oil

2tsp of wholegrain mustard

1. Fill two-thirds of the large saucepan with water and bring it to the boil. Season with a pinch of salt, add the pasta, and **boil** for 12–14 minutes.

2. When the pasta has been cooking for about 6–7 minutes add the green beans to the pan. Finish cooking and drain the pasta and beans in a colander.

3. **Refresh** the pasta and beans with cold water. Drain the tuna, using a sieve and then use your fingers to break the tuna into small flakes.

Pasta cooking times vary, so make sure that you check the packet.

Chef's tip
Check out p.14–15
for more information
on hard-boiling eggs.
And see p.125 for
more egg tips.

4. Hard-boil the eggs for 6–7 minutes and put them in cold water. Tap the cooled eggs to crack the shell. **Peel** the eggs and cut them into wedges.

5. Spoon the olive oil, white wine vinegar, and mustard into a jar. Screw the lid on tightly and shake vigorously to mix the dressing ingredients together.

6. Mix the pasta with half of the dressing. **Fold** in the tomatoes, beans, tuna, onions, olives, and remaining dressing. Season and serve with some wedges of egg.

Cheese and potato pasties

Puff pastry is really difficult to make at home so even some of the best chefs buy it ready-made! It is really versatile and can be used for sweet or savoury pies and pasties.

Tools

- ❑ small saucepan
- ❑ slotted spoon
- ❑ frying pan or sauté pan
- ❑ wooden spoon
- ❑ saucer or small plate (approx 12cm/5" in diameter)
- ❑ knife
- ❑ mixing bowl
- ❑ metal mixing spoon
- ❑ fork
- ❑ pastry brush
- ❑ oven gloves
- ❑ large non-stick baking tray

Recipe idea
Try other fillings such as spinach, mushroom, or bacon, but make sure that you cook them in steps 1 and 2. You could even try a sweet filling, such as the apple pie mixture from p.116–117, but the apples should be finely chopped.

Ingredients for 8 pasties

250g (8oz) potatoes (peeled and diced)

1 pinch of salt

1tbsp of olive oil

2 x 375g (12oz) ready-rolled puff pastry sheets

1 onion (peeled and diced)

250g (8oz) cheddar cheese (grated)

flour (for rolling)

1 egg (for glazing)

salt and pepper

Food fact
Brushing the pasties with beaten egg gives the pastry a golden glaze when it is cooked. You could also use milk for this.

Serving tip
Allow the pasties to cool for at least 5 minutes before you eat them because they will be really hot!

1. Preheat the oven to 220°C (425°F/Gas 7). Half-fill a pan with water and bring to the boil. Add the potato and a pinch of salt and bring back to the boil.

2. **Par-boil** the potato for 5–7 minutes and then drain it. Heat the oil and gently **fry** the onion for 2 minutes, to soften. Leave the onion and potato to cool.

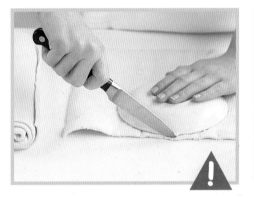

3. Unroll the pastry sheets onto a lightly-floured surface. Using an upside-down saucer or small plate as a template, cut out 8 circles of pastry.

4. Put the cooled potato and onion into a bowl and add the cheese. **Mix** them all together with a metal spoon and season with salt and pepper.

5. Beat the egg lightly with a fork. Brush the edges of each pastry circle with the beaten egg. This will help the pastry to stick together.

6. Place some of the cheese and potato mixture in the centre of each pastry circle. Bring the edges together to enclose the filling and form a semi-circle.

7. Gently **crimp** the edges by pinching the pastry in opposite directions. **Glaze** the pasties with beaten egg and bake for 20 minutes or until golden.

Falafel with tzatziki

Falafel are spicy chick pea patties and they originally came from the Middle East. Chick peas are part of a food group called pulses which are a good source of protein, vitamins, and minerals and are also high in fibre.

Tools
- ❑ food processor
- ❑ medium frying pan
- ❑ slotted metal spatula
- ❑ plate
- ❑ kitchen paper
- ❑ grater
- ❑ chopping board
- ❑ t-towel or cloth
- ❑ small bowl
- ❑ mixing bowl
- ❑ dessert spoon

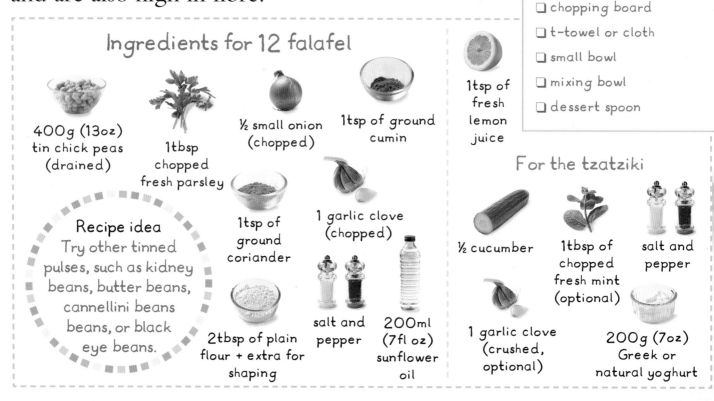

Ingredients for 12 falafel

400g (13oz) tin chick peas (drained)

1tbsp chopped fresh parsley

½ small onion (chopped)

1tsp of ground cumin

1tsp of fresh lemon juice

Recipe idea
Try other tinned pulses, such as kidney beans, butter beans, cannellini beans beans, or black eye beans.

1tsp of ground coriander

1 garlic clove (chopped)

2tbsp of plain flour + extra for shaping

salt and pepper

200ml (7fl oz) sunflower oil

For the tzatziki

½ cucumber

1tbsp of chopped fresh mint (optional)

salt and pepper

1 garlic clove (crushed, optional)

200g (7oz) Greek or natural yoghurt

1. Put the chick peas, onion, garlic, cumin, coriander, flour, parsley, and seasoning into the processor and **blend** them together until smooth.

2. Lightly flour the work surface and tip out the mixture. Divide it into 12 equal portions and **shape** each portion into a flat, round patty.

3. Pour the oil into the frying pan and heat it over a medium-high heat. **Shallow fry** the falafel for 2–3 minutes on each side, or until golden and crisp.

Serving tip
The falafel and tzatziki taste great by themselves or served with pitta bread!

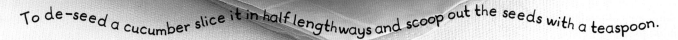

To de-seed a cucumber slice it in half lengthways and scoop out the seeds with a teaspoon.

4. Take the cooked falafel out of the frying pan with a slotted metal spatula. Place them on a plate lined with kitchen paper to drain the excess oil.

5. **De-seed** and then **grate** the cucumber. Wrap the cucumber in a clean t-towel or cloth and firmly squeeze out any excess moisture, over a small bowl.

6. **Mix** together the grated cucumber, yoghurt, lemon juice, mint, and garlic. Season with salt and pepper and serve the tzatziki with the falafel.

• **preparation** 30 minutes   • **chilling** at least 1 hour   • **cooking** 20 minutes

Sushi rolls

Impress your friends with these sophisticated sushi rolls. Once you have mastered the rolling technique in steps 5–7, they are quite simple. This recipe makes 4 long rolls with a carrot or cucumber filling which you can then cut up into delicious bite-sized pieces.

Tools

- ❑ medium saucepan with lid
- ❑ serving spoon
- ❑ wooden spoon
- ❑ small saucepan
- ❑ shallow dish (approx. 15cm x 20cm/6" x 8")
- ❑ cling film
- ❑ chopping board
- ❑ teaspoon
- ❑ sharp knife
- ❑ bamboo sushi mat or squares of cling film
- ❑ plate

Serve the sushi with a side dish of soy sauce, for dipping.

Recipe idea
Experiment with alternative sushi fillings such as tuna, salmon, crabmeat, cheese, avocado, or peppers.

Ingredients for 4 long rolls

250g (8oz) sushi rice (rinsed)

1tbsp of caster sugar

325ml (11fl oz) water

½ tsp of table salt

2tbsp of rice wine vinegar

4 seaweed (nori) sheets

For the fillling

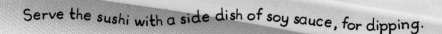

½ small cucumber (halved lengthways)

or

½ carrot (peeled and halved lengthways)

For dipping

soy sauce

1. Add the rice and water to the pan and cover with a lid. Bring to the boil and then reduce the heat. **Simmer** for 10 minutes. Remove the pan from the heat.

2. Leave the covered rice to stand for 10 minutes or until the liquid has been absorbed. Meanwhile, **warm** the vinegar, sugar, and salt until dissolved.

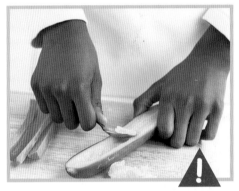

3. Line a shallow dish with cling film. Stir the sweetened vinegar mixture into the rice then carefully pack it into the dish. Leave to cool.

4. **De-seed** the cucumber, using a teaspoon and then **slice** it into 4 equal strips. If you are using a carrot instead, cut it into 4 long strips.

Serving tip
Put the rolls onto a plate, cover with cling film, and chill for at least 1 hour. When the rolls are ready, rinse a sharp knife under cold water and slice them into 5 or 6 pieces.

5. Place a nori sheet, shiny side down, onto a bamboo mat. Dip your hands in water and pat a quarter of the rice so that it covers two-thirds of the nori.

6. Lay a piece of cucumber or carrot widthways along the centre of the rice. Holding the mat, **roll** the nori over and over, to the edge of the rice.

7. Tuck the rolled edge of the nori firmly under the filling. Dampen the remaining nori and roll it up. Using the mat, pull the sushi roll tightly to seal.

Main meals

It is vital to have one substantial main meal every day. Most people have their main meal at the end of the day when they have more time to prepare and enjoy it. If you have your main meal in the evening, it is important not to eat just before you go to bed as your food will not be properly digested and a full stomach might keep you awake!

There is nothing more satisfying than eating something that you have prepared yourself! In this section you will find some of your favourite recipes but you will also be able to experiment with new ingredients and types of food as well as learning some new cooking skills.

Noodle soup

This is a healthy, filling, and complete meal in a bowl. Best of all, it only uses one saucepan so there is less to wash up afterwards!

1. Heat the vegetable oil in a medium saucepan. Gently **fry** the spring onions over a medium heat for 1–2 minutes, or until soft.

Ingredients for 2 servings

2tsp of vegetable oil

2 spring onions (trimmed and sliced diagonally)

1 thin slice of fresh ginger, peeled (optional)

juice of ½ lime

600ml (1pt) fish stock (made with ⅓ of stock cube)

75g (2½oz) fine egg noodles

1tsp of soy sauce

60g (2oz) baby corn (halved)

60g (2oz) sugar snap peas

125g (4oz) ready-to-cook raw prawns (shelled)

1 drop of sesame oil

2tsp of chopped fresh coriander (optional)

Tools
❑ medium saucepan
❑ wooden spoon
❑ measuring jug

2. Stir the ginger, stock, lime juice, and soy sauce into the spring onion and bring to the boil. Lower the heat and then **simmer** for 2–3 minutes.

3. Remove the ginger. Add the noodles and corn and bring to the boil. After 1½ minutes, add the sugar snap peas and cook for a further 1½ minutes.

4. Lower the heat to bring the soup back to a simmer. Stir in the prawns and cook them for 2–3 minutes, or until pink. Stir in the sesame oil and coriander.

Raw prawns are grey or white in colour but they turn pink when they are cooked!

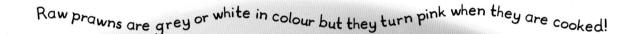

Food fact
Do not overcook the prawns because it makes the texture rubbery! And if you are using frozen prawns, make sure that you defrost them completely before cooking them.

● **preparation** 15–20 minutes ● **cooking** 10–15 minutes

Chicken wraps

The combination of red and yellow peppers and green mange tout make these wraps look really colourful and the simple flavouring gives the chicken a refreshing zingy taste. See p.123 for tips on how to check whether your chicken is cooked properly.

Tools
- ❑ 2 chopping boards
- ❑ vegetable knife
- ❑ sharp knife
- ❑ medium bowl
- ❑ small whisk
- ❑ wooden spatula
- ❑ large frying pan
- ❑ tongs
- ❑ ovenproof plate
- ❑ kitchen foil
- ❑ oven gloves

Don't overcook the vegetables – they taste better slightly crunchy!

Ingredients for 8 wraps

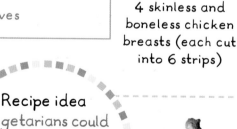
4 skinless and boneless chicken breasts (each cut into 6 strips)

1 small yellow pepper

1 small red pepper

125g (4oz) mange tout

8 flour tortillas

juice of ½ lime

Recipe idea
Vegetarians could use tofu instead of chicken or double the amount of vegetables.

2.5cm (1") fresh ginger, peeled and grated (optional)

For the flavouring

2tbsp of clear runny honey

1 pinch of salt

1tbsp of sunflower oil

3–4 dashes of pepper sauce (optional)

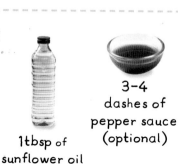

Serving tip
Chicken wraps taste great served with a dollop of guacamole (see p. 30–31) and sour cream on the side.

1. Preheat the oven to 200°C (400°F/Gas 6). **De-seed** both peppers and slice them into 12 equal strips. (See p.122 for expert tips on this.)

2. **Mix** the oil, honey, ginger, pepper sauce, and salt together, in a bowl. Stir in the chicken strips until they are completely coated with the flavouring.

3. Heat the frying pan for 2 minutes. Add the coated chicken and **fry** it for 4–5 minutes. The chicken will turn golden and then caramelize.

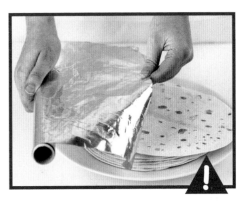

4. Place the tortillas on the ovenproof plate and cover with foil. Put them in the preheated oven for 6–7 minutes, or until they are warmed through.

Chef's tip
In step 5 the chicken and vegetables will continue to cook in the hot frying pan, so serve immediately or transfer them to a serving dish.

5. Add the peppers, mange tout, and lime juice to the chicken. Cook for 4–5 minutes on a medium–high heat. Stir occasionally to prevent sticking.

6. Lay some of the filling along the top of each tortilla, leaving the other end and sides empty. If you over-fill your tortilla, you will not be able to wrap it.

7. To wrap, fold the empty end inwards and overlap the sides. The filling should be securely wrapped but peeping out appetisingly from the open end!

Peperoni pasta

This delicious recipe provides a wide range of nutrients, from carbohydrates in the pasta to protein in the sausage, and vitamins in the tomatoes and peppers.

Tools
- ☐ chopping board
- ☐ sharp knife
- ☐ garlic crusher
- ☐ 2 large saucepans
- ☐ wooden spoon
- ☐ slotted metal spoon
- ☐ colander
- ☐ pasta spoon

Ingredients for 4-6 servings

2 garlic cloves

1 red onion

1tsp of dried oregano

2 red peppers (roasted, peeled, and de-seeded)

125g (4oz) peperoni

200ml (7fl oz) vegetable stock

4 dashes of pepper sauce (optional)

2tbsp of sun-dried tomato paste

400g (13oz) tin chopped tomatoes

1tsp of Worcestershire sauce (optional)

1tbsp of caster sugar

salt and pepper

75g (2½oz) per person spaghetti

1tbsp of olive oil

10 fresh basil leaves (torn)

Recipe idea
Any type of cooked or cured sausage would taste delicious in this recipe and if you don't have sun-dried tomato paste, tomato purée will be fine.

1. **Dice** the red onion and roasted peppers. Peel and **crush** the garlic cloves. (See p.122 for expert dicing and crushing tips.)

2. Cut the peperoni into diagonal slices, about 1.5cm (¾") thick. Add the oil to the saucepan and heat it over a medium heat.

3. **Sauté** the onion for 2–3 minutes. Add the garlic and oregano and cook for 1–2 minutes. Add the peperoni and cook for a further 2 minutes.

A sprinkling of freshly grated Parmesan cheese adds extra flavour.

Serving tip
Use the pasta spoon to transfer the spaghetti into pasta bowls. Season the sauce and serve it on top of the spaghetti.

4. Add the tomatoes, tomato paste, peppers, sugar, stock, Worcestershire and pepper sauces. Bring to the boil and then **simmer** for 20 minutes.

5. Half-fill a large saucepan with water and bring it to the boil. Add a pinch of salt then lower the spaghetti into the pan, using a slotted spoon.

6. Boil the pasta for 10–12 minutes (check the exact timings on the pack). Drain the pasta and then stir the fresh basil into the tomato sauce.

Barbecue chicken

Marinating is a simple but effective way of adding extra flavour to meat, fish, and vegetables. Soaking these chicken pieces in a marinade for at least an hour before you cook them gives them a delicious barbecue taste. On a warm summer's day, they could be cooked on an outdoor barbecue.

Tools

- ❏ small mixing bowl
- ❏ whisk
- ❏ large dish (approx. 5cm/2" deep)
- ❏ kitchen paper
- ❏ sharp knife
- ❏ chopping board
- ❏ cling film
- ❏ oven gloves
- ❏ foil-lined grill tray
- ❏ tongs
- ❏ dessert spoon

Ingredients for 4 servings

8 chicken drumsticks

2tbsp of tomato ketchup

2tbsp of soy sauce

3tbsp of clear runny honey

2tbsp of fresh orange juice

1tbsp of sunflower oil

1 garlic clove (crushed)

1tsp of mustard

Recipe idea
Chicken breasts or thighs also taste great cooked this way but always check that the meat is completely cooked. (See p.123 for tips on this.)

1. Put all the ingredients except the chicken drumsticks in a bowl and **whisk** them together. Pour the mixture into a large, shallow dish.

2. Pat the chicken pieces with kitchen paper. Make 3 deep cuts in each drumstick. This is known as **scoring** and helps the meat to soak up the marinade.

3. Put the chicken in the dish and roll each piece until it is coated with sauce. Cover with cling film and leave to **marinate** in the refrigerator for 1 hour.

Wrap the cooled chicken in a napkin and eat with your fingers!

Safety tip
You must always wash your hands thoroughly after touching raw meat to avoid spreading any germs.

Serving tip
The chicken will need to stand for 2–3 minutes before you are ready to serve it.

4. Preheat the **grill** to a medium heat. Lay the coated chicken (uncut-side up) on a foil-lined grill tray. Put the marinade to one side.

5. Grill the chicken pieces for 7–8 minutes. Using tongs, turn the chicken over and grill the other side for a further 7–8 minutes.

6. Turn the chicken again. Spoon over half the sauce. Grill for 5 minutes, turn, and spoon over the rest of the sauce. Grill for a final 5 minutes.

● **preparation** 35–40 minutes   ● **cooking** 15–20 minutes

Chicken curry

Curry originally came from Asia, and this recipe is influenced by the fragrant curries of Thailand. For an Indian-style curry, use double the amount of the paste from p.34–35 and miss out step 1.

Tools
- ❏ chopping board
- ❏ sharp knife
- ❏ food processor
- ❏ wok or large saucepan
- ❏ wooden spoon
- ❏ medium saucepan with lid
- ❏ measuring jug

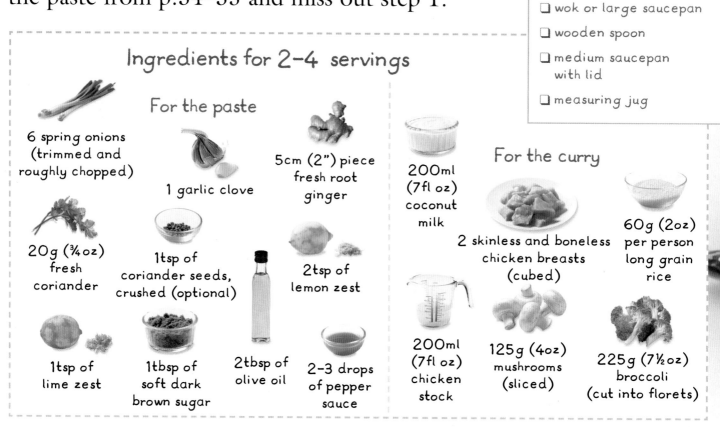

Ingredients for 2–4 servings

For the paste

6 spring onions (trimmed and roughly chopped)

1 garlic clove

5cm (2") piece fresh root ginger

20g (¾oz) fresh coriander

1tsp of coriander seeds, crushed (optional)

2tsp of lemon zest

1tsp of lime zest

1tbsp of soft dark brown sugar

2tbsp of olive oil

2–3 drops of pepper sauce

200ml (7fl oz) coconut milk

For the curry

2 skinless and boneless chicken breasts (cubed)

200ml (7fl oz) chicken stock

125g (4oz) mushrooms (sliced)

60g (2oz) per person long grain rice

225g (7½oz) broccoli (cut into florets)

1. **Peel** and **chop** the ginger. Roughly chop the garlic and fresh coriander. Put all the paste ingredients into a processor and **blend** until smooth.

2. Place a wok or saucepan over a medium heat. Pour in half of the coconut milk and stir in half of the paste. Cook for 1 minute, stirring constantly.

3. Add the chicken and cook it for 3–4 minutes. Rinse the rice with cold water and tip it into a saucepan. Add double the amount of water to the rice.

For extra zing, you could add green or red chillies instead of the pepper sauce in step 1.

Safety tip
Although the chicken will change colour, it will not be completely cooked in step 3.

4. Cover the rice and bring it to the boil. **Simmer** until all the water is absorbed. If the rice is not quite cooked, add water and cook for a few more minutes.

5. While the rice is cooking, add the remaining coconut milk and paste to the wok. Add the stock, stir, and then boil for 1 minute. Reduce the heat to a simmer.

6. Add the mushrooms and simmer for 1 minute. Then add the broccoli and simmer for a further 4–5 minutes. Serve with the cooked rice.

● preparation 20 minutes ● cooking 15–20 minutes

Stir-fry with noodles

Stir-frying is a quick way to cook – the ingredients are stirred continually over a high heat for a short amount of time so the vegetables remain crunchy. This recipe is made with tofu, a great alternative to meat that is high in protein and calcium.

Tools

- [ ] medium saucepan with lid
- [ ] kitchen paper
- [ ] chopping board
- [ ] sharp knife
- [ ] jug
- [ ] whisk
- [ ] wok or large frying pan
- [ ] wooden spatula
- [ ] plate
- [ ] tongs
- [ ] colander
- [ ] pasta spoon

Recipe idea
Chicken or prawns could be used instead of tofu but make sure you cook them thoroughly in step 4.

Ingredients for 2–4 servings

250g (8oz) firm tofu

2 spring onions (trimmed)

1 carrot (peeled)

1 red pepper (de-seeded)

2tsp of sunflower oil

60g (2oz) baby corn

75g (2½oz) per person dried medium egg noodles

60g (2oz) unsalted cashew nuts (optional)

60g (2oz) sugar snap peas

For the stir-fry sauce

1tsp of clear runny honey

1tbsp of fresh orange juice

1tsp of sesame oil

1tbsp of soy sauce

2tbsp of sunflower oil

1. Half-fill a medium saucepan with water, cover, and bring to the boil. Drain the tofu and pat it dry with kitchen paper. Cut the tofu into cubes.

2. Diagonally **slice** the spring onions. Cut the carrot in half and then into long sticks. Slice the pepper into strips and cut the corn in half.

Food fact
Cooking vegetables for only a short time means that they retain most of their nutrients, which can sometimes be lost through over-cooking.

3. To make the stir-fry sauce, **whisk** the honey, orange juice, sesame oil, sunflower oil, and soy sauce together in a small jug until they are fully mixed in.

4. Heat half of the oil and fry the tofu over a high heat for 7 minutes, or until golden. Take it out of the wok and place it on a plate lined with kitchen paper.

5. Lower the noodles into the boiling water. Bring the pan back to the boil and cook the noodles for 4 minutes or as instructed on the packet.

6. Use the remaining oil to **stir-fry** the spring onions, carrot, and pepper for 2–3 minutes. Add the corn, nuts, peas, and sauce. Stir-fry for 2 minutes.

7. Add the cooked tofu and stir-fry for a further 2 minutes. Drain the noodles and serve the stir-fried vegetables and tofu over the noodles.

● **preparation** 25–30 minutes ● **cooking** 1 hour

Mashed potato pies

This recipe is a tasty variation on a traditional cottage pie. It is a filling and nutritious main meal and can easily be made with beef, pork, lamb, or vegetarian mince. If you don't have four small dishes, you can use one large dish instead.

Tools
❑ chopping board
❑ peeler
❑ sharp knife
❑ garlic crusher
❑ 2 large saucepans
❑ wooden spoon
❑ colander
❑ masher
❑ four ovenproof dishes
❑ large baking tray
❑ slotted spoon
❑ teaspoon
❑ dessert spoon
❑ oven gloves

Recipe idea
These pies can also be made using vegetarian mince and vegetable stock for a meat-free alternative.

Always use oven gloves to handle hot dishes.

Ingredients for 4 pies

1tbsp of olive oil

1 carrot

1 onion

2tsp of chopped rosemary leaves (optional)

500g (1lb) lean minced beef

1 garlic clove

1tbsp of tomato purée

150ml (¼pt) beef stock

125g (4oz) mushrooms (quartered)

2tsp of Worcestershire sauce (optional)

salt and pepper

400g (13oz) can chopped tomatoes

For the topping

550g (1lb 2oz) potatoes

1 pinch of salt

2tbsp of milk

30g (1oz) unsalted butter

75g (2½oz) cheese (grated)

1. Preheat the oven to 200°C (400°F/Gas 6). **Peel** and **dice** the onion and carrot. **Crush** the garlic. (See p.122 for expert cutting and crushing tips.)

2. Heat the oil and **fry** the beef for 4 minutes or until browned, stirring constantly. Add the onion, carrot, rosemary, and garlic and fry for 3–5 minutes.

3. Add the mushrooms, stock, tomato purée, Worcestershire sauce, and tomatoes. Bring to the boil and then reduce to a **simmer** for 20 minutes. Season.

4. Half-fill a pan with water and bring it to the boil. Peel and chop the potatoes and add them to the pan, with the salt. Boil for 12–15 minutes, or until soft.

Serving tip
Allow the pies to cool for a few minutes before eating them. They taste great served with vegetables, such as broccoli or peas.

5. Drain the potatoes in a colander and then tip them back into the saucepan. **Mash** the potatoes with the milk, butter, and half of the cheese.

6. Place the dishes on a baking tray and divide the meat filling equally between them, using a slotted spoon. Top each with a quarter of the mashed potato.

7. Sprinkle the remaining cheese on top of the mashed potato and bake the pies for 25–30 minutes, or until they are golden and bubbling.

Meatballs with salsa

Give classic meatballs a sweet and sour twist with this tasty recipe. Grilling is healthier than frying, and using skewers makes it much safer and easier to cook the meatballs evenly. When using skewers, you must soak them in water for at least 1 hour so that they don't splinter or burn during cooking.

Tools

- ❑ bread knife
- ❑ chopping board
- ❑ food processor
- ❑ 2 large mixing bowls
- ❑ wooden spoon
- ❑ plate
- ❑ cling film
- ❑ dessert spoon
- ❑ 6 wooden skewers
- ❑ oven gloves
- ❑ grill rack and foil-lined tray
- ❑ fork
- ❑ bowl

Chilling the meatballs before cooking stops them from falling apart.

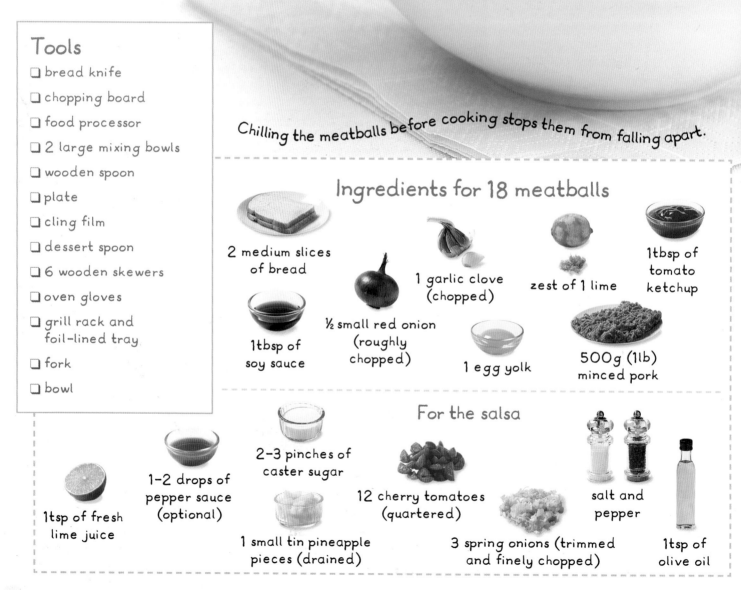

Ingredients for 18 meatballs

2 medium slices of bread

1 garlic clove (chopped)

zest of 1 lime

1tbsp of tomato ketchup

1tbsp of soy sauce

½ small red onion (roughly chopped)

1 egg yolk

500g (1lb) minced pork

For the salsa

1tsp of fresh lime juice

1–2 drops of pepper sauce (optional)

2–3 pinches of caster sugar

12 cherry tomatoes (quartered)

1 small tin pineapple pieces (drained)

3 spring onions (trimmed and finely chopped)

salt and pepper

1tsp of olive oil

1. Cut the crusts off and tear the bread into chunks. Put the bread into the food processor and **blend** it until it becomes fine breadcrumbs.

2. Tip the breadcrumbs into a bowl. Put the onion and garlic into the food processor and finely blend them. Add them to the bowl of breadcrumbs.

Chef's tip
For traditional-style meatballs, use the mixture from the hamburger recipe on p.40-41 and follow these steps. You could even serve them with the tomato sauce (without the peperoni!) and spaghetti from p.56-57.

3. Add the meat, lime zest, tomato ketchup, soy sauce, and egg yolk to the bowl. Using a wooden spoon or your fingers, **mix** until fully combined.

4. Using your hands, **shape** the meat mixture into 18 equal balls. Place the meatballs on a plate, cover with cling film, and chill them for 30 minutes.

5. Put the pineapple into a mixing bowl and stir in the spring onions, tomatoes, lime juice, pepper sauce, sugar, and olive oil. Season and set aside.

6. Preheat the grill to a medium heat. Carefully place 3 meatballs on each skewer. **Grill** them for 14–16 minutes, turning them every 3–4 minutes.

7. When the meatballs are cooked completely, use a fork to slide them carefully off the skewers. Serve the meatballs with some salsa on the side.

Lamb kebabs

This marinade adds a gentle spicy flavour to the lamb while the cous cous is very simple to cook and is a great alternative to rice.

Tools

- ❑ 2 mixing bowls
- ❑ dessert spoon
- ❑ cling film
- ❑ chopping board
- ❑ sharp knife
- ❑ 8 wooden skewers
- ❑ oven gloves
- ❑ grill rack and foil-lined tray
- ❑ tongs
- ❑ fork

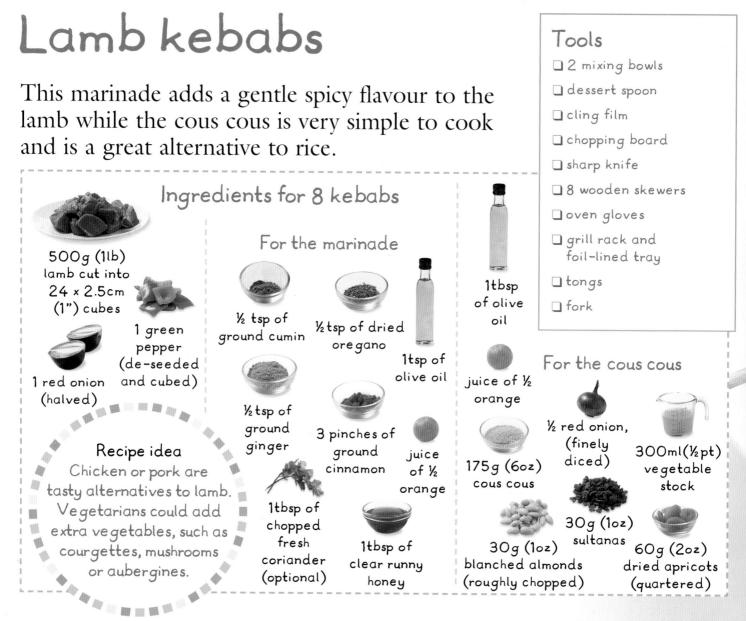

Ingredients for 8 kebabs

500g (1lb) lamb cut into 24 x 2.5cm (1") cubes

1 green pepper (de-seeded and cubed)

1 red onion (halved)

Recipe idea
Chicken or pork are tasty alternatives to lamb. Vegetarians could add extra vegetables, such as courgettes, mushrooms or aubergines.

For the marinade

½ tsp of ground cumin

½ tsp of dried oregano

1tsp of olive oil

½ tsp of ground ginger

3 pinches of ground cinnamon

juice of ½ orange

1tbsp of chopped fresh coriander (optional)

1tbsp of clear runny honey

1tbsp of olive oil

For the cous cous

juice of ½ orange

175g (6oz) cous cous

½ red onion, (finely diced)

300ml (½pt) vegetable stock

30g (1oz) blanched almonds (roughly chopped)

30g (1oz) sultanas

60g (2oz) dried apricots (quartered)

1. **Mix** all of the marinade ingredients together in a bowl. Stir in the lamb and cover with cling film. Leave to **marinate** for 1–2 hours in the fridge.

2. Cut each onion half into 4 equal wedges and remove the white core from each piece. Split the wedges in half to make 16 thin pieces of onion.

3. Place a cube of lamb onto a skewer, followed by pieces of onion and pepper. Repeat and add a piece of lamb to finish. Do the same for all 8 skewers.

Chef's tip
Soak the wooden skewers for at least 1 hour before you use them so that they don't burn or splinter in step 4.

Serving tip
Serve the kebabs on a bed of cous cous. Cous cous also tastes great on its own, so you could miss out the second part of step 6.

4. Preheat the grill to a medium heat. **Grill** the kebabs for 12–16 minutes, turning every 2–3 minutes. Allow to rest before serving.

5. Meanwhile, pour the hot stock over the cous cous and mix them together. Cover the bowl with cling film until all the liquid has been absorbed.

6. Fluff the cooked cous cous with a fork to separate the grains. Stir in the orange juice, onion, apricots, almonds, sultanas, and olive oil.

Roasted vegetable lasagne

For this recipe, it is important to use the type of dried lasagne that does not need pre-cooking. Check the packet to make you sure that you buy the right kind! Fresh lasagne would also be fine but you would have to reduce the cooking time.

Tools

☐ chopping board

☐ sharp knife

☐ roasting tin

☐ oven gloves

☐ large saucepan

☐ wooden spoon

☐ small saucepan

☐ whisk

☐ lasagne dish
  (approx 25cm x 18cm
  and 5cm deep or
  10" x 7" and 2" deep)

☐ serving spoon

Recipe idea
For an alternative filling, try the meat mixture from the Mashed potato pies on p. 64–65.

Ingredients for 6–8 servings

2 large red onions

2 large carrots (peeled)

2 large courgettes

2 red peppers (de-seeded)

1 medium aubergine

2tsp of chopped fresh rosemary

1 tbsp of tomato purée

2 yellow peppers (de-seeded)

400g (13oz) can chopped tomatoes

9 dried lasagne sheets

salt and pepper

2 garlic cloves (crushed)

4tbsp of olive oil

For the sauce

500ml (17fl oz) warm milk

60g (2oz) unsalted butter

30g (1oz) plain flour

salt and pepper

125g (4oz) Parmesan cheese (grated)

1. Preheat the oven to 220°C (425°F/Gas 7). Cut the onions into wedges and then **chop** the carrots, courgettes, aubergine, and peppers into chunks.

2. In the roasting tin, **mix** the oil, rosemary, and garlic with the vegetables and season. **Roast** for 35 minutes, shaking the tin occasionally.

3. Gently **warm** the tomatoes and tomato purée through in a large saucepan. Take the pan off the heat and carefully stir in the roasted vegetables.

4. Over a low heat, melt the butter in a small pan. Stir in the flour for 1 minute and **whisk** in the milk. Stir until thickened. Add half the cheese and season.

Chef's tip
If your sauce goes lumpy in step 4, don't worry! Sieve out the lumps, before you add the cheese.

5. Lower the oven to 190°C (375°F/Gas 5). Spoon a third of the vegetables into the base of the lasagne dish and top with 3 lasagne sheets.

6. Add another third of the vegetables and pour over half the sauce. Top with another layer of lasagne sheets and add the remaining vegetables.

7. Finally add the 3 remaining lasagne sheets and sauce. Sprinkle the cheese over the top and bake for 35 minutes or until golden and bubbling.

Tuna fishcakes

Like all oily fish, tuna contains vitamins and minerals that are good for the brain, skin, and eyes. This recipe involves shallow frying, like the falafel in p.46–47. This gives the fishcakes a crispy, golden coating but it is important to drain them on kitchen paper in step 6 to remove the excess oil.

Tools

- ❑ medium saucepan
- ❑ colander
- ❑ masher
- ❑ mixing bowl
- ❑ fork
- ❑ large plate
- ❑ cling film
- ❑ dish
- ❑ 2 medium plates
- ❑ medium sauté or frying pan
- ❑ slotted metal spatula
- ❑ kitchen paper

Ingredients for 8 fishcakes

250g (8oz) potatoes (peeled and chopped)

1 pinch of salt

350g (11½oz) tinned tuna (drained weight)

2tsp of Dijon mustard

1 spring onion (trimmed and finely chopped)

salt and pepper

2 eggs

2tsp of chopped fresh parsley

90g (3oz) plain flour

150g (5oz) breadcrumbs (approx 7 slices, without crusts)

200ml (7fl oz) vegetable oil

To serve

salad leaves

lemon or lime wedges

1. Half-fill the saucepan with water. Add the potato and a pinch of salt. Bring the water to the boil and cook for 12–15 minutes or until soft.

2. Thoroughly drain the potatoes and put them back into the pan. **Mash** the potatoes and leave them to one side until they are cool enough to handle in step 4.

3. Break the tuna into small pieces in a bowl. Stir in the mashed potato, mustard, spring onion, and parsley until they are fully mixed in. Season.

Use tuna in spring water or brine rather than oil, because it is lower in fat.

Chef's tip
Fry the fishcakes in batches of 2 or 4 and keep the cooked ones warm in the oven. Serve with salad and lemon or lime wedges.

4. Lightly dust your hands with flour and **shape** the mixture into 8 cakes. Place the fishcakes on a plate, cover with cling film, and chill for 30 minutes.

5. **Beat** the eggs together in a dish and put the breadcrumbs and flour on separate plates. **Coat** each fishcake in flour, egg, and then breadcrumbs.

6. Heat the oil over a medium heat. **Shallow fry** the cakes for 2 minutes on each side, or until golden. Drain them on a plate lined with kitchen paper.

● **preparation** 20-25 minutes　● **standing** 30 minutes (optional)　● **cooking** 30-35 minutes

Sausage popovers

The secret to good popovers is to make sure that the oil is very hot in step 3 before you add the sausages and then the batter in step 4. Leaving the batter to stand for half an hour before cooking also helps to give the popovers a lighter texture.

Tools

- ❑ sieve
- ❑ mixing bowl
- ❑ ramekin
- ❑ whisk
- ❑ oven gloves
- ❑ non-stick 12-hole muffin tray
- ❑ tongs
- ❑ ladle
- ❑ small saucepan
- ❑ wooden spoon
- ❑ small plate

Ingredients for 12 popovers

1 pinch of salt

3 eggs

4tbsp of vegetable oil

250ml (8fl oz) milk

1tsp of snipped fresh chives (optional)

150g (5oz) plain flour

1tbsp of wholegrain mustard (optional)

4 long sausages (each cut into 3 pieces)

For the onion gravy

1tbsp of vegetable oil

1tsp of dark brown soft sugar

1tsp of balsamic vinegar (optional)

1 small red onion (thinly sliced)

15g (½oz) unsalted butter

300ml (½pt) beef stock

1tbsp of plain flour

Chef's tip
For a plain popover, leave out the chives, mustard, and sausage. Heat the oil in the tray, as in step 3, and cook the batter for 18–20 minutes.

Serving tip
Pour the onion gravy over the popovers and serve with vegetables, such as peas. Sieve the gravy if you prefer a smoother sauce.

1. Preheat the oven to 220°C (425°F/Gas 7). **Sieve** the flour and salt into a bowl and make a hole in the centre. **Crack** the eggs and add them, one by one.

2. Using a whisk, **beat** the milk into the eggs and flour until you have a smooth batter, with no lumps. Stir in the chives and mustard (optional).

3. Add 1tsp of oil to each muffin hole and heat the tray in the oven for 3 minutes. Take the hot tray out of the oven and add some sausage to each hole.

4. Put the tray back into the oven for 4 minutes. Remove the tray and half-fill each hole with batter. Put it back in the oven and cook for 18–20 minutes.

5. Meanwhile, heat the oil in the saucepan and stir in the onion, sugar, and vinegar. Gently cook the onion for 10 minutes until soft and browned.

6. Spoon the onion out of the pan onto a plate and melt the butter in the same pan. Add the flour and stir for 30 seconds, or until browned.

7. Add the stock and bring it to the boil. Boil for 1 minute, and then add the onion. Lower the heat and then **simmer** for 10 minutes, or until thickened.

● **preparation** 25–30 minutes ● **cooking** 1 hour 20 minutes

Roast chicken

Everyone loves an old-fashioned roast dinner! With this easy-to-follow recipe, you can produce a meal to be proud of. Make sure you read the recipe carefully and check that the chicken is cooked properly in steps 5 and 6. See p.123 for advice on how to check if your meat is cooked.

Tools

- ❑ chopping board
- ❑ kitchen paper
- ❑ small mixing bowl
- ❑ 2 dessert spoons
- ❑ sharp knife
- ❑ string
- ❑ roasting tin
- ❑ oven gloves
- ❑ rack
- ❑ tray
- ❑ carving knife
- ❑ carving fork

Ingredients for 4 servings

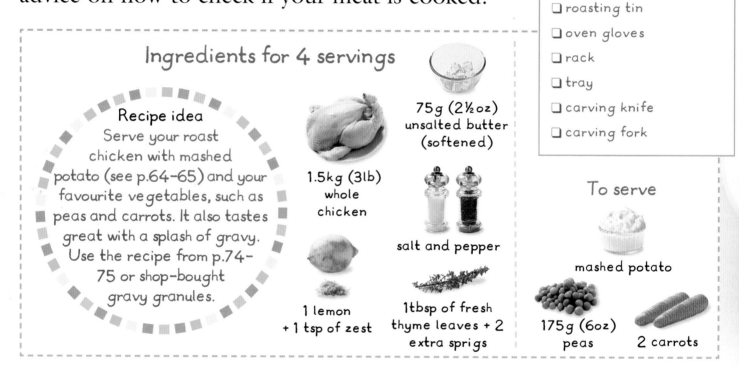

Recipe idea
Serve your roast chicken with mashed potato (see p.64–65) and your favourite vegetables, such as peas and carrots. It also tastes great with a splash of gravy. Use the recipe from p.74–75 or shop-bought gravy granules.

1.5kg (3lb) whole chicken

1 lemon + 1 tsp of zest

75g (2½oz) unsalted butter (softened)

salt and pepper

1tbsp of fresh thyme leaves + 2 extra sprigs

To serve

mashed potato

175g (6oz) peas

2 carrots

1. Preheat the oven to 200°C (400°F/Gas 6). Rinse inside the chicken with cold water. Place it on a board and pat it dry, inside and out, with kitchen paper.

2. To make the stuffing, **mix** the softened butter with the thyme leaves, lemon zest, salt, and pepper in a bowl until it forms a smooth mixture.

3. Lift the skin at the top of the breastbone and slide your hand in to form pockets on either side. Stuff half of the flavoured butter into each pocket.

Chef's tip
Tying the chicken's legs together in step 4 helps the chicken to keep its shape during cooking. You should also tuck the wing tips underneath.

4. Cut the zested lemon in half. Place one half inside the chicken, with the thyme sprigs. Tie the legs together with string and put the chicken into a roasting tin.

5. Season the chicken and **roast** it for 1 hour 20 minutes, or until golden brown. **Baste** the meat after 30 minutes and then every 15 minutes after that.

6. Carefully transfer the cooked chicken to a rack (over a tray to catch any drips) and leave to rest for 10–15 minutes before carving and serving.

Desserts

The desserts in this section have been specially created so that they taste great and provide lots of essential nutrients. Desserts containing milk and other dairy products are good sources of protein and an important mineral called calcium, while fruit-based desserts supply vitamins and minerals.

This section introduces you to some new techniques, from whipping and whisking to melting and meringue-making. Don't forget to read the recipes through thoroughly before you begin and check out the glossary on p.122-125 for tips.

Yoghurt ices

You can use your favourite flavours to make this alternative to ice cream. What a great way to cool down on a hot summer's day!

1. Carefully **chop** the fudge and honeycomb into tiny pieces and break the cookies into slightly larger pieces. Leave to one side.

Ingredients for 8-12 scoops

150ml (¼pt) double cream

30g (1oz) icing sugar

500g (1lb) natural yoghurt

90g (3oz) chocolate cookies

90g (3oz) soft fudge

60g (2oz) mini marshmallows

60g (2oz) honeycomb (optional)

Recipe idea
Try out this recipe with 300g (10oz) of your favourite ingredients, e.g. bananas, strawberries, meringues (see p.92-93), chocolate chips, or chopped up bars of chocolate.

Tools
- ❏ chopping board
- ❏ sharp knife
- ❏ mixing bowl
- ❏ sieve
- ❏ whisk
- ❏ spatula or metal spoon
- ❏ 2 plastic tubs with lids

2. Pour the cream into the mixing bowl and **sieve** in the icing sugar. Lightly **whip** the cream to soft peaks. (You could use an electric or hand whisk.)

3. Gently **fold** the yoghurt honeycomb, fudge, cookies, and marshmallow pieces into the cream using a plastic spatula or metal spoon.

4. Spoon the mixture into the tubs, cover, and freeze. Stir the mixture after 2 hours to prevent ice crystals forming and then freeze for at least 2 more hours.

Serving tip
When the mixture is completely frozen, allow it to soften for a few minutes before serving. Scoop out and serve on wafer cones or in bowls. Do not re-freeze.

Fruit pops

Make your own delicious frozen lollipops with this simple mix-and-match recipe. Create colourful combinations with layers of fruit, yoghurt, and pure juice. These lollipops are an excellent source of vitamins and they are a great way to cool down on a hot summer's day!

Tools
- [ ] sharp knife
- [ ] chopping board
- [ ] food processor
- [ ] sieve
- [ ] wooden spoon
- [ ] 2 mixing bowls
- [ ] 6 lollipop moulds
- [ ] 6 lollipop sticks
- [ ] teaspoon

Ingredients for 6 lollipops

Recipe idea
Any of your favourite fruits or fruit juices would taste great in this recipe. Try stirring 100g (3½ oz) strawberries into 300g (10oz) of flavoured yoghurt to make 4 creamy lollipops.

300g (10oz) strawberries

300ml (½pt) orange juice

3 large kiwi fruits

3tbsp of icing sugar

1. First, rinse and drain the strawberries in cold water. Then **hull** and quarter the strawberries and put them into a food processor.

2. Cut a thin slice off the top and bottom of each kiwi fruit. Working from top to bottom, carefully **slice** the skins off and then roughly chop the kiwis.

3. In a food processor, **blend** the strawberries with 1tbsp of the icing sugar. **Sieve** the strawberry purée into a bowl and throw away the seeds.

Serving tip
If you have any problems getting the lollipops out of the moulds, run them under the tap.

4. Wash the food processor and sieve. Blend the kiwi fruit with 2tbsp of icing sugar. Sieve the kiwi purée into a bowl and throw away the seeds.

5. Add the first layer and freeze for 1 hour to set. Add the next layer and push the stick gently into the first layer. Freeze for 1 hour and add the last layer.

6. Do not fill the moulds right to the top as the mixture will expand a little as it freezes. Freeze the lollipops for a final 1–2 hours before eating.

Chocolate fridgecake

This fridgecake looks great but it is actually very simple because unlike most cakes, it doesn't involve any baking! It is a tempting mixture of melt-in-your-mouth chocolate, crumbly biscuit, chewy cherries, and crunchy nuts.

Tools
- ❑ cling film
- ❑ loaf tin (500g/1lb)
- ❑ 2 medium mixing bowls
- ❑ small saucepan
- ❑ wooden spoon
- ❑ chopping board
- ❑ sharp knife
- ❑ oven gloves
- ❑ rubber spoon spatula
- ❑ dessert spoon

Ingredients for 10-12 servings

200g (7oz) plain chocolate

125g (4oz) unsalted butter

1tbsp of golden syrup

150g (5oz) plain biscuits

90g (3oz) red glacé cherries (optional)

60g (2oz) shelled pistachio nuts (optional)

60g (2oz) raisins (optional)

30g (1oz) blanched almonds (optional)

Recipe idea
You could miss out the cherries, raisins, and nuts if you want and replace them with the same quantity of puffed rice, marshmallows, or other dried fruits.

1. Tear off a piece of cling film, at least double the size of the loaf tin. Loosely **line** the tin with the cling film and then put the tin to one side.

2. Break the chocolate into a bowl and add the butter and syrup. Place the bowl over a pan of barely simmering water and gently **melt** the contents.

3. Halve the cherries and break the biscuits into small pieces. If you would prefer a smoother fridgecake, break the biscuits into even smaller pieces.

When the fridgecake has softened, cut it into 10-12 equal slices.

4. Using oven gloves, remove the chocolate from the heat, and allow the bowl to cool slightly. Stir in the remaining ingredients until coated.

5. Spoon the mixture into the loaf tin and press it down with the back of a spoon. Loosely cover with the extra cling film and chill for 2 hours, to set.

6. Carefully turn the tin upside down on a chopping board. Remove the tin and unwrap the cling film. Leave the fridgecake to soften for a few minutes.

Mandarin cheesecake

This scrumptious cheesecake looks amazing but is simple to make. The filling is a mixture of cream cheese, condensed milk, and lemon juice and the base is just made of crushed biscuits and a little melted butter. Best of all, this cheesecake does not need any baking, just chilling.

Tools
- [ ] plastic food bag
- [ ] rolling pin
- [ ] medium saucepan
- [ ] wooden spoon
- [ ] flan tin (20cm/8", loose bottomed and fluted)
- [ ] baking tray
- [ ] dessert spoon
- [ ] mixing bowl
- [ ] rubber spoon spatula
- [ ] balloon whisk
- [ ] colander
- [ ] chopping board
- [ ] knife

Ingredients for 8-10 servings

200g (7oz) digestive biscuits

75g (2½oz) unsalted butter

200g (7oz) cream cheese, at room temperature

300g (10oz) sweetened condensed milk

5tbsp of fresh lemon juice

300g (10oz) tin mandarin segments in natural juice

Recipe idea
Other tinned fruits would taste great in this recipe. Try cherries, peaches, pineapple, or a combination of your favourite fruits.

1. Break up the biscuits and put them into a food bag. Push the air out and seal. **Crush** the biscuits with a rolling pin until they are like fine breadcrumbs.

2. Gently **melt** the butter in a saucepan, over a low heat. Turn off the heat and stir in the crushed biscuits until they are completely coated with butter.

3. Put the flan tin on a baking tray and tip the biscuit mixture in. Spread the mixture out with the back of a spoon until it evenly covers the base and sides.

Chef's tip
For a really
naughty-but-nice
dessert, sprinkle some
grated chocolate
on top of the
cheesecake.

4. Chill the biscuit base for 30 minutes. **Beat** the cream cheese and then add the condensed milk and lemon juice. **Whisk** them all together, until smooth.

5. Thoroughly drain the mandarin segments. Roughly chop them into smaller pieces and then scatter them over the chilled biscuit base.

6. Pour the filling mixture over the base. Use a spatula to spread the mixture and smooth the top. Chill for 2–3 hours or overnight, to set.

● **preparation** 20 minutes   ● **cooking** none

Summer fruit ripple

This creamy, light dessert looks great and tastes delicious! Although this recipe suggests fresh fruit, frozen fruit would be fine, but you must thaw it completely before you begin. On a hot summer's day, you can freeze the finished ripple for at least 4 hours, to make a super-cool treat.

Tools
- [ ] chopping board
- [ ] sharp knife
- [ ] food processor
- [ ] sieve
- [ ] 2 mixing bowls
- [ ] wooden spoon
- [ ] dessert spoon
- [ ] balloon whisk
- [ ] metal mixing spoon
- [ ] rubber spoon spatula

Ingredients for 4 servings

250g (8oz) ripe strawberries

125g (4oz) ripe raspberries

125g (4oz) ripe blueberries

4tbsp of fresh orange juice

275ml (9fl oz) natural yoghurt

Recipe idea
Try using tinned fruit such as mangoes and peaches but remember to set some fruit aside for decoration.

275ml (9fl oz) double cream

2tbsp of clear runny honey

2tbsp of icing sugar (sieved)

1. Wash all the fruit and put a handful to one side. (They will be used to decorate the finished dessert.) **Hull** the strawberries and cut them into quarters.

2. Place the orange juice, icing sugar, and half of the fruit into the processor. Put the lid on securely and **blend** to make a smooth purée.

3. **Sieve** the blended fruit into a mixing bowl to separate the seeds and fruit pulp. Use a wooden spoon to press the liquid through.

If you don't have a food processor use a masher to crush the fruit in step 2.

Serving tip
To serve, place the fruit set aside in step 1 on top of the rippled mixture in the serving glasses.

4. Carefully stir the rest of the strawberries, blueberries, and raspberries into the fruit purée with a metal spoon (excluding the fruits set aside in step 1!)

5. Lightly **whip** the cream in the large bowl. When it is ready, it will stand up in soft peaks. (You can use an electric whisk here, if you have one.)

6. Fold the yoghurt, honey, and half of the fruit mixture into the cream. Layer the marbled cream mixture with the rest of the fruit mixture, in serving glasses.

● **preparation** 30 minutes   ● **cooking** 30–35 minutes

Fruit crumble

Crumble is a traditional English dessert and it tastes great served with cream, ice cream, or custard. Like all fruits, blackberries and peaches are a good source of vitamins, while the oats used in the crumble topping provide carbohydrates and fibre.

Tools
- ☐ chopping board
- ☐ sharp knife
- ☐ teaspoon
- ☐ 2 mixing bowls
- ☐ metal mixing spoon
- ☐ sieve
- ☐ wooden spoon
- ☐ ovenproof dish (approx. 23 x 15 cm and 5cm deep or 9 x 6" and 2" deep)
- ☐ baking tray
- ☐ oven gloves

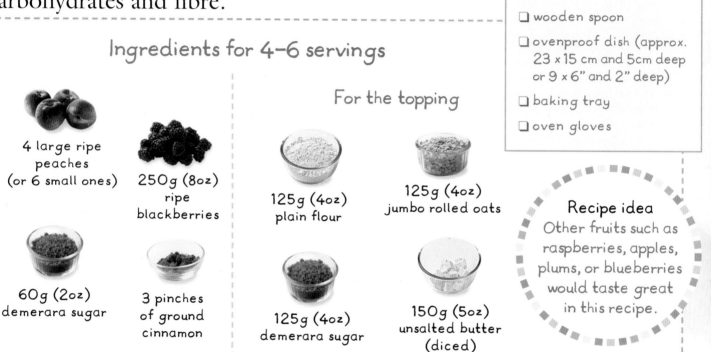

Ingredients for 4-6 servings

4 large ripe peaches (or 6 small ones)

250g (8oz) ripe blackberries

60g (2oz) demerara sugar

3 pinches of ground cinnamon

For the topping

125g (4oz) plain flour

125g (4oz) jumbo rolled oats

125g (4oz) demerara sugar

150g (5oz) unsalted butter (diced)

Recipe idea
Other fruits such as raspberries, apples, plums, or blueberries would taste great in this recipe.

1. Preheat the oven to 190°C (375°F/Gas 5). Cut round the peaches and then twist them so that they split in half. Scoop the stones out with a teaspoon.

2. Slice the halved peaches in half again and then **chop** each piece into three more chunks. Rinse and thoroughly drain the blackberries.

3. Mix the sugar and cinnamon together in a bowl. **Fold** in the peaches and blackberries until they are completely coated in the sugar mixture.

If your fruit is not ripe, you may need to add more sugar in step 3.

Safety tip
Leave the crumble to stand for 10 minutes before serving. It will still be warm, but cool enough to eat!

4. **Sieve** the flour into a separate bowl and stir in the demerara sugar. Add the oats to the bowl and stir them into the flour and sugar.

5. Using your fingertips, **rub** the diced butter into the flour mixture. The mixture should come together in small lumps when it is ready.

6. Place the dish on a baking tray and spoon in the fruit filling. Scatter the topping over and **bake** the crumble for 30 minutes or until golden.

● preparation 40–45 minutes   ● cooking 2 hours

Tropical fruit meringues

Here's a handy tip – egg whites are easier to whisk when they are at room temperature. You should also use a clean, grease-free glass bowl when making meringues and ensure that the whites are completely free from any yolk.

Tools

- ☐ baking sheet
- ☐ non-stick baking parchment
- ☐ large bowl
- ☐ electric whisk
- ☐ tablespoon
- ☐ metal mixing spoon
- ☐ 2 dessert spoons
- ☐ oven gloves
- ☐ chopping board
- ☐ sharp knife
- ☐ large mixing bowl

Add some meringue pieces in step 6 of the Fruit Ripple (p.88–89).

Ingredients for 12 meringues

2 eggs

125g (4oz) caster sugar

1 pinch of salt

For the fruit salad

½ small melon (quartered and deseeded)

1 kiwi fruit

2tbsp of fresh orange juice

1 small mango

10 red grapes (halved)

10 green grapes (halved)

½ small pineapple

Recipe idea
You can use any of your favourite fruits in the salad – apple, peach, or banana would all taste great.

1. Preheat the oven to 110°C (225°F/Gas ½) and **line** a baking sheet with non-stick parchment. **Separate** the egg whites from the yolks. (See p.125 for tips.)

2. **Whisk** the egg whites and salt in a large bowl, until they form stiff peaks. Whisk 5tbsp of the sugar into the mixture, 1tbsp at a time.

Chef's tip
Cooked meringues will be dry and should peel off the baking parchment very easily.

3. Make sure the egg whites are stiff before adding each tablespoon of sugar. **Fold** the remaining sugar into the mixture, using a metal spoon.

4. Using 2 dessert spoons, put 12 spoonfuls of the meringue onto the baking sheet and bake on the bottom shelf of the oven for 2 hours.

5. Carefully **slice** the mango in half, around the stone. Slice the skin from the melon. Scoop out the mango and melon flesh and cut them into cubes.

6. Prepare the pineapple and kiwi. First cut off the top and bottom and then slice off the skin, working downwards. Cut out the core from the pineapple.

7. Cut the kiwi into slices and the pineapple into cubes. Mix all the fruit together and stir in the orange juice. Chill until the meringues are ready.

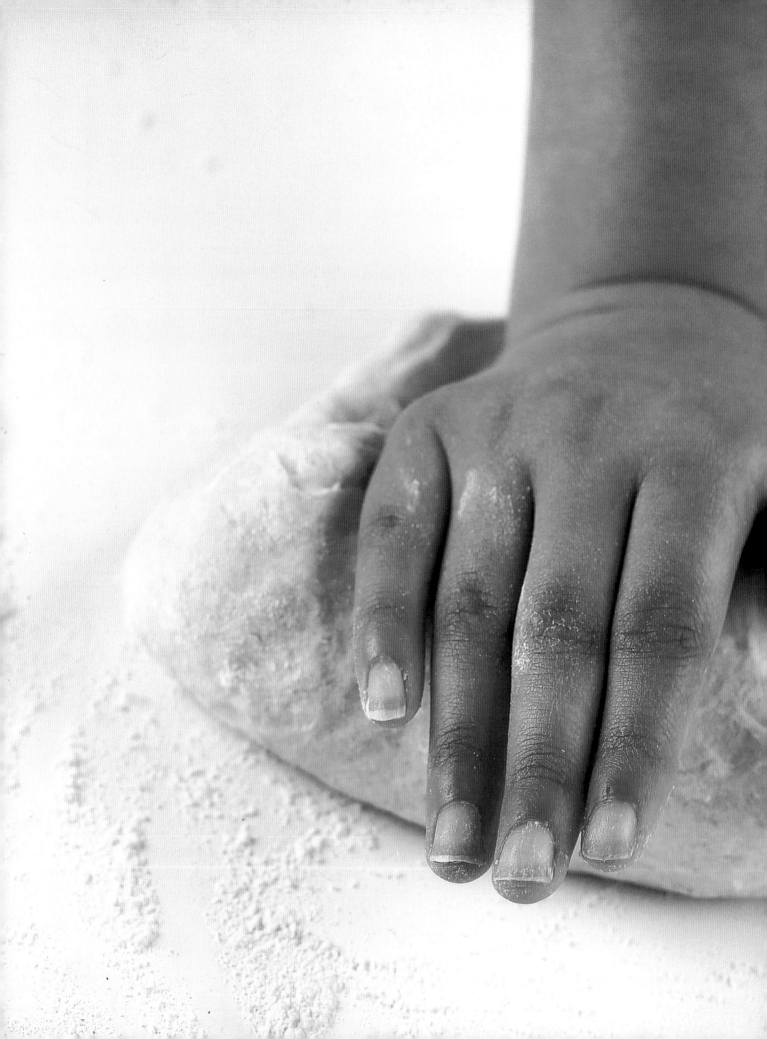

Baking

There is nothing quite like the smell of a homemade cake or loaf of bread baking in the oven! Bread is a good source of carbohydrates but cakes and biscuits can be high in fat and sugar. However, as long as your diet is healthy, it is fine to eat a little of your favourite foods!

Baking is a lot of fun and you will learn some specialist skills in this section, from rubbing and kneading to rolling and creaming. The recipes contain lots of handy tips and advice so you should read them very carefully before you start baking. Make sure that you ask for help from an adult if you need it and refer to the glossary on p.122-125 for extra advice.

● preparation 30-35 minutes   ● cooking 25 minutes

Crunchy muffins

The secret of delicious, light muffins is not to over-mix the cake batter. A few lumps don't matter – if the batter is over-mixed, the muffins will have a heavy, dense texture.

Ingredients for 12 muffins

300g (10oz) plain flour

1tbsp of baking powder

½ tsp of salt

125g (4oz) granulated sugar

1 egg

2tbsp of corn oil or sunflower oil

275ml (9fl oz) milk

90g (3oz) crunchy oat cereal

125g (4oz) fresh raspberries

150g (5oz) white chocolate (chopped)

Recipe idea
Frozen raspberries would be fine for this recipe, as long as you thaw them completely. Try using other fresh or frozen fruits, such as strawberries, blueberries, or blackberries. Nuts, dried fruits, or chocolate chips would also taste great!

1. Preheat the oven to 200°C (400°F/Gas 6). **Sieve** the plain flour, baking powder, and salt into a mixing bowl and then stir in the sugar.

2. **Crack** the egg into a jug and add the oil. **Beat** the egg and oil together until they are light and fluffy. Add the milk and then **whisk** the mixture.

3. **Fold** the egg mixture into the flour mixture. The mixture will be lumpy but no flour should be visible. Then fold in the chocolate and raspberries.

Don't worry if the raspberries break up in step 3. The muffins will still taste delicious!

4. Put the muffin cases into the muffin tray and spoon the mixture into them. The easiest way is with a dessert spoon and the back of a teaspoon.

5. Sprinkle some of the crunchy oat cereal on top of each muffin. Bake the muffins for 25 minutes, or until risen and golden.

6. Remove the muffins from the oven and allow them to cool in the muffin tray before placing them on a wire rack. Then you can help yourself!

medium 2

● preparation 20-25 minutes   ● cooking 25 minutes

Chocolate brownies

Here are a few tips on baking brownies – melt the chocolate gently over a low heat and make sure that the bowl does not touch the water in the pan. You must fold, not stir, the mixture in step 5, and you should always line the tin to prevent the brownies sticking to it.

Tools

- ☐ baking tin (20cm x 15cm or 8" x 6")
- ☐ scissors
- ☐ pencil
- ☐ baking parchment
- ☐ 3 medium bowls
- ☐ wooden spoon
- ☐ small saucepan
- ☐ sieve
- ☐ rubber spoon spatula
- ☐ palette knife
- ☐ oven gloves

Ingredients for 12-16 brownies

90g (3oz) plain chocolate

150g (5oz) unsalted butter + extra for greasing

125g (4oz) plain flour

15g (½oz) cocoa powder

 1tsp of vanilla extract

 ½ tsp of baking powder

Recipe idea
If you don't like nuts or are allergic to them, you can leave them out. These brownies taste just as delicious without nuts.

 300g (10oz) soft light brown sugar

 1 pinch of salt

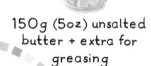 2 eggs

100g (3½oz) chopped pecan nuts (optional)

1. Preheat the oven to 180°C (350°F/Gas 4). **Grease** and **line** the base of the baking tin with non-stick baking parchment.

2. Break the chocolate into a bowl and add the butter. **Melt** the butter and chocolate over a saucepan of barely simmering water, stirring occasionally.

3. Remove the bowl from the heat and allow the chocolate to cool slightly. **Sieve** the flour, cocoa powder, baking powder, and salt into a separate bowl.

Chef's tip
A brownie should be firm on the outside but gooey and fudge-like on the inside.

4. In a third bowl, **beat** the eggs and then add the sugar and vanilla extract. Stir the ingredients together until they are just combined.

5. Fold the melted chocolate into the beaten egg mixture. Then fold in the flour mixture and nuts. There should be no visible flour.

6. Spoon the mixture into the tin, smooth the top with a palette knife, and bake for 25 minutes. Allow it to cool in the tin before cutting into squares.

● **preparation** 35 minutes ● **cooking** about 40 minutes

Chocolate cookies

This is a versatile recipe for melt-in-your-mouth cookies. You can use either chocolate spread for a double chocolate taste or peanut butter for a nutty flavour.

Ingredients for 20 cookies

125g (4oz) unsalted butter (softened)

90g (3oz) soft light brown sugar

1 egg

125g (4oz) chocolate spread

30g (1oz) cocoa powder

2-3 drops of vanilla extract

90g (3oz) caster sugar

200g (7oz) plain flour

150g (5oz) white chocolate chips

1 pinch of salt

½ tsp of baking powder

Recipe idea
For a nutty cookie, miss out the cocoa powder in step 3, swap the chocolate spread for the same amount of peanut butter in step 2, and use plain chocolate chips instead.

1. Preheat the oven to 180°C (350°F/Gas 4). **Cream** the butter and both types of sugar together in a large bowl until the mixture turns creamy.

2. Still using the electric whisk, **beat** the egg, chocolate spread, and vanilla extract into the creamed butter and sugar mixture, until fully mixed in.

3. **Sieve** the flour, baking powder, cocoa powder, and salt into a bowl. Use a wooden spoon to help the mixture through, if you need to.

Chef's tip
For best results, bake the trays of cookies one at a time, on the middle shelf of the oven.

You can use milk, white, or plain chocolate chips or even a mixture!

4. Add the sieved flour mixture to the chocolate mixture and gently **mix** them together with a wooden spoon. Stir in the chocolate chips.

5. Place 6–7 heaped dessert spoonfuls of the cookie dough onto each baking tray, leaving space between each mound so they can spread as they cook.

6. Bake for 14 minutes. Take the trays out of the oven and leave the cookies to set for 2–3 minutes. When set, transfer them onto a cooling rack.

● **preparation** 30 minutes ● **cooking** 35 minutes

Banana squares

The melt-in-your mouth texture of this cake is due to the creaming and folding and the use of buttermilk (or yoghurt) which make the mixture light and airy. Adding the fresh banana in step 3 also makes the cake deliciously moist.

Tools
☐ pencil
☐ square cake tin (20cm/8")
☐ non-stick baking parchment
☐ scissors
☐ 2 large mixing bowls
☐ electric whisk
☐ sieve
☐ wooden spoon
☐ step palette knife
☐ oven gloves
☐ medium frying pan
☐ wooden spatula
☐ plate
☐ cooling rack

To make muffins, bake the mixture in a muffin tray for 25-30 mins.

Recipe idea
For a plain and simple cake, leave out the topping, or try some whipped cream instead.

Ingredients for 12-16 squares

125g (4oz) unsalted butter (softened) + extra, for greasing

125g (4oz) soft light brown sugar

200g (7oz) self-raising flour

1tsp of baking powder

500g (1lb) ripe bananas (peeled and mashed)

2 eggs (beaten)

1 pinch of salt

2tbsp of buttermilk or natural yoghurt

For the topping
(optional)

200g (7oz) cream cheese (room temperature)

60g (2oz) icing sugar (sifted)

60g (2oz) desiccated coconut

1. Preheat the oven to 180°C (350°F/Gas 4). With a pencil, draw round the tin onto the parchment paper. Cut out the square. **Grease** and **line** the tin.

2. **Cream** the butter and sugar together in a large bowl until light and fluffy. Gradually **beat** the eggs into the creamed butter and sugar mixture.

3. **Sieve** the flour, salt, and baking powder into the creamed mixture and gently **fold** them in. Next, stir in the banana and buttermilk.

4. Spoon the cake mixture into the prepared tin and smooth the top with a palette knife. Bake the cake in the oven for 35 minutes, or until firm.

Chef's tip
Allow the cake to cool in the tin for 5-10 minutes in step 4 before gently turning it out on to the cooling rack.

5. Meanwhile, **dry fry** the coconut over a low heat until golden, stirring continuously. Tip the toasted coconut onto a plate to stop it from burning.

6. Beat the cheese and icing sugar together with a wooden spoon until completely combined. It should become smooth, soft, and spreadable.

7. When the cake is completely cool, cut it into squares. Add a spoonful of the cream cheese topping and a sprinkling of toasted coconut to each square.

● preparation 30–35 minutes   ● rising about 2½ hours   ● cooking 30–35 minutes

Homemade bread

It is simple to create a light, airy loaf of bread. All you need are a few basic ingredients – flour, yeast, salt, and water. The most important thing is to learn special bread-making skills, such as kneading and knocking back. These are all explained in the glossary on p.124.

Tools

☐ ramekin
☐ sieve
☐ mixing bowl
☐ wooden spoon
☐ large bowl
☐ cling film
☐ 2 loaf tins (500g/1lb)
☐ pastry brush
☐ oven gloves

Food fact
Yeast helps the bread to rise and gives it a light texture.

Recipe idea
If you don't have fresh yeast, you can use 7g (⅓ oz) of easy-blend dry yeast instead. Miss out step 1 and stir the dry yeast and 1tsp of caster sugar into the sieved flour in step 2.

Ingredients for 2 loaves

250ml (8fl oz) lukewarm water

1tbsp of olive oil (+ extra for greasing)

15g (½oz) fresh yeast

1tsp of caster sugar

450g (14½oz) strong plain white bread flour, plus extra for kneading

2tsp of salt

For the topping

2tsp of poppy seeds (optional)

1 egg (beaten)

2tsp of sesame seeds (optional)

Chef's tip
The dough needs to be put in a warm, but not hot, place to rise. Places such as an airing cupboard or near a warm oven are perfect!

1. Using your finger, mix 3tbsp of the water with the yeast and sugar. Leave it in a warm place for 10 minutes or until it begins to bubble.

2. **Sieve** the flour and salt into a bowl and stir in the yeast mixture. Stir in the oil and then enough of the remaining water to make a soft dough.

3. Lightly flour your hands and the work surface. **Knead** the dough for about 10 minutes or until it becomes smooth and elastic. (See p.124 for tips.)

4. Put the dough in a lightly-greased bowl and cover it with greased cling film. Put it in a warm place for 1½ hours, until the dough has doubled in size.

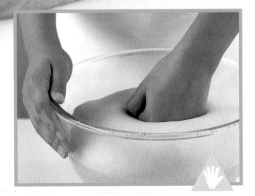

5. Preheat the oven to 220°C (425°F/Gas 7). **Knock back** the risen dough and then knead it on a lightly-floured surface for a further 5 minutes.

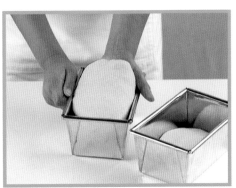

6. Shape the dough into 2 rectangles. Place each piece into a lightly-greased loaf tin, cover and put them in a warm place until they have doubled in size.

7. **Glaze** the loaves with egg and sprinkle with seeds. Bake for 30–35 minutes. A cooked loaf will look golden and sound hollow if tapped on the base.

● **preparation** 40–45 minutes   ● **rising** about 1 hour   ● **cooking** 4–6 minutes

Naan bread

Naan is a special type of flatbread from India that is usually eaten with curry. Unlike the loaf of bread on p.104–105, naan bread is grilled not baked. As the naan cooks, a hollow pocket forms inside which is perfect for adding a tasty filling, as on p.34–35.

Tools
- ❑ ramekin
- ❑ sieve
- ❑ wooden spoon
- ❑ 2 large bowls
- ❑ cling film
- ❑ table knife
- ❑ rolling pin
- ❑ baking tray
- ❑ pastry brush
- ❑ oven gloves

The dough will be sticky in step 3 so rub a little flour on your hands.

Recipe idea
If you are using dry yeast, miss out step 1 and stir in 5g (¼oz) of easy-blend dry yeast in step 2.

Ingredients for 4 naans

3 tbsp of warm milk

2 tsp of fresh yeast

200g (7oz) strong plain white bread flour

½ tsp of salt

2 tsp of cumin seeds (optional)

1 egg (beaten)

vegetable oil (for greasing)

3 tbsp of natural yoghurt

30g (1oz) unsalted butter (melted)

1. Using your finger, mix the milk and fresh yeast together in a ramekin. Leave the mixture in a warm place for 10 minutes or until it bubbles slightly.

2. **Sieve** the flour and salt into a bowl. Using a wooden spoon, gradually stir the yeast mixture, egg, and yoghurt into the flour until you have a soft dough.

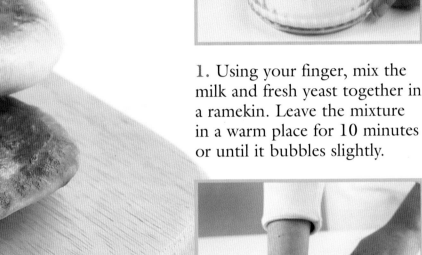

Chef's tip
The milk in step 1 should be lukewarm, not hot. If it is too hot, it will kill the yeast and the bread will not rise.

3. On a lightly-floured surface, **knead** the dough for 5 minutes or until it is smooth and elastic. Lightly grease a bowl with oil and then add the dough.

4. Cover the bowl with lightly-greased cling film and leave it in a warm place for about 1 hour or until the dough has doubled in size.

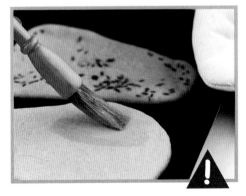

5. Remove the cling film and **knock back** the dough. Divide the dough into 4 equal pieces and knead some of the cumin seeds into each piece (optional).

6. **Roll** each piece into a teardrop shape. Don't be afraid to stretch the dough to get the right shape! Preheat the baking tray under a hot grill.

7. Place the naan breads on the hot baking tray and **glaze** both sides with melted butter. **Grill** each side on high for 2 minutes or until risen and golden.

● **preparation** 60 minutes   ● **rising** 1–1½ hours   ● **cooking** 20–25 minutes

Pizza

The pizza base is made in the same way as the bread on p.104–105. However, the dough only needs to rise once in this recipe, rather than twice, like the bread.

Tools

☐ ramekin
☐ 2 sieves
☐ mixing bowl
☐ 2 wooden spoons
☐ large bowl
☐ cling film
☐ small bowl
☐ small saucepan
☐ teaspoon
☐ chopping board
☐ rolling pin
☐ baking tray
☐ dessert spoon
☐ oven gloves

Ingredients for 2 pizzas

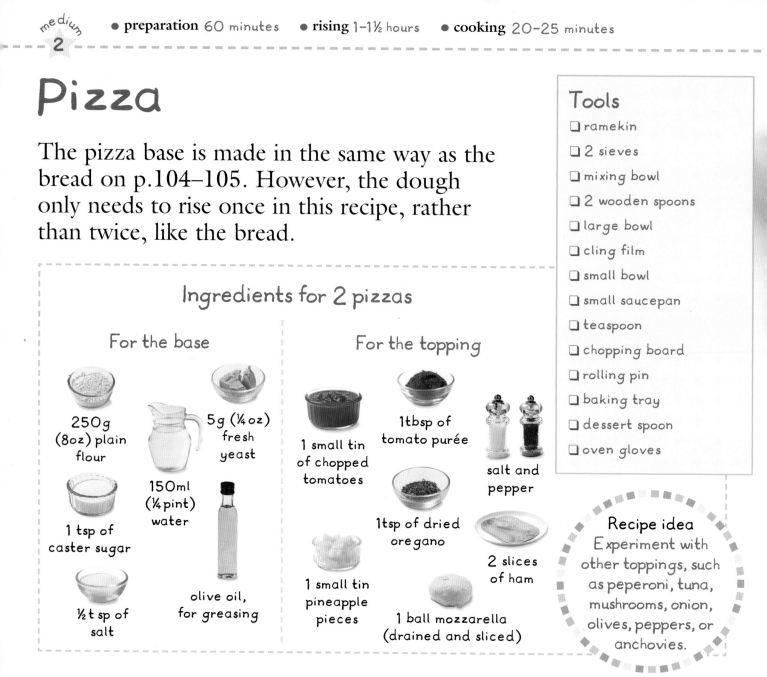

For the base

250g (8oz) plain flour

150ml (¼ pint) water

5g (¼oz) fresh yeast

1 tsp of caster sugar

½ tsp of salt

olive oil, for greasing

For the topping

1 small tin of chopped tomatoes

1tbsp of tomato purée

salt and pepper

1tsp of dried oregano

1 small tin pineapple pieces

2 slices of ham

1 ball mozzarella (drained and sliced)

Recipe idea
Experiment with other toppings, such as peperoni, tuna, mushrooms, onion, olives, peppers, or anchovies.

1. To make the base, follow steps 1–4 on p.104–105. While the dough is rising in step 4, use a sieve to drain the excess liquid from the tomatoes.

2. Put the tomatoes into a small saucepan and add the tomato purée, oregano, salt, and pepper. Gently **warm** them over a low heat for 2 minutes.

3. With your fingers, tear the ham and mozzarella into bite-sized pieces. Drain the pineapple pieces. Preheat the oven to 220°C (425°F/Gas 7).

Pesto is a tasty alternative to tomato sauce on a pizza. (See p. 36–37 for a recipe.)

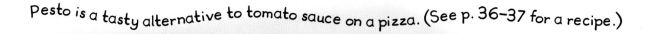

Chef's tip
To prevent sticking and to make 2 equal-sized circles in step 4, turn the dough 45° after each roll.

4. Knock back the risen dough and put it onto a lightly-floured work surface. **Roll** it out into 2 equal circles, about 15cm (6") in diameter.

5. Place the pizza bases on a lightly-greased baking tray. Spread half of the tomato onto each base leaving a 2cm (¾") rim around the edge.

6. Add the toppings and bake the pizzas for 20–25 minutes. Let the pizzas cool a little before cutting and eating as the cheese will be very hot!

● preparation 30 minutes ● chilling 15 minutes ● cooking 20 minutes

Strawberry shortbreads

These strawberry shortbreads are a perfect way to impress your family and friends. You can bake them a couple of days in advance and store them in an airtight container. When you are ready, whip up the toppings and serve the shortbread.

Tools
- [ ] mixing bowl
- [ ] electric whisk
- [ ] sieve
- [ ] fork
- [ ] cling film
- [ ] greaseproof paper
- [ ] rolling pin
- [ ] cookie cutter
- [ ] large baking tray
- [ ] oven gloves
- [ ] small saucepan
- [ ] dessert spoon
- [ ] cooling rack

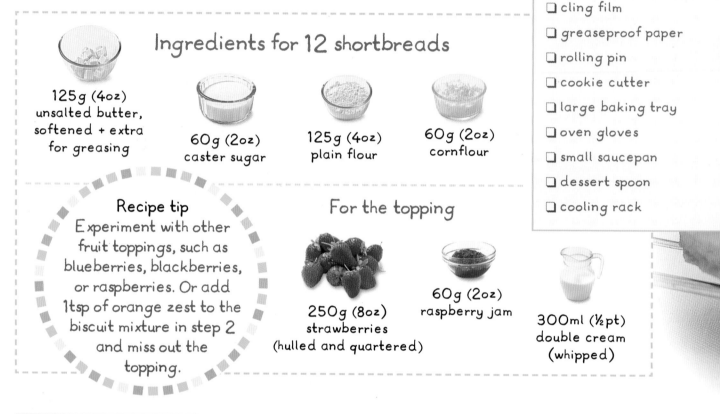

Ingredients for 12 shortbreads

125g (4oz) unsalted butter, softened + extra for greasing

60g (2oz) caster sugar

125g (4oz) plain flour

60g (2oz) cornflour

Recipe tip
Experiment with other fruit toppings, such as blueberries, blackberries, or raspberries. Or add 1tsp of orange zest to the biscuit mixture in step 2 and miss out the topping.

For the topping

250g (8oz) strawberries (hulled and quartered)

60g (2oz) raspberry jam

300ml (½pt) double cream (whipped)

1. Preheat the oven to 170°C (325°F/Gas 3). Place the butter and sugar in a bowl and **cream** together until light and fluffy using an electric whisk.

2. **Sieve** the plain flour and cornflour into the creamed butter. **Mix** together with a fork until all the ingredients are combined.

3. Form the dough into a smooth, round disc, using your hands. Wrap the dough in cling film and leave it to chill in the fridge for 15 minutes.

Experiment with different shaped cookie cutters eg. hearts, flowers, or stars.

Serving tip
Add a generous dollop of whipped cream to each biscuit and top with a spoonful of the strawberries.

4. Place the chilled dough between 2 pieces of greaseproof paper. **Roll** it out to form a circle, about 20cm (8") in diameter and 1cm (½") thick.

5. Cut out 12 shortbreads and place them onto a greased baking tray. (You will need to gather and re-roll the dough a few times.) Bake for 20 minutes.

6. In a pan **warm** the jam, fold in the strawberries, and leave to cool. Take the shortbreads out of the oven and allow them to set in the tray. Put them onto a rack.

● **preparation** 15 minutes ● **chilling** 1½ hours ● **cooking** 7-9 minutes

Orange crunch biscuits

These tangy biscuits just melt in your mouth! They can be served with icing for a tasty treat or plain for a simple homemade biscuit.

Tools
- ❏ sieve
- ❏ 2 mixing bowls
- ❏ table knife
- ❏ cling film
- ❏ 2 baking sheets
- ❏ knife
- ❏ oven gloves
- ❏ cooling rack
- ❏ wooden spoon
- ❏ piping bag and nozzle or teaspoon

If you don't have a piping bag, use a spoon to drizzle the icing.

Recipe idea
Try using 1tsp of lemon zest or ground ginger instead of orange zest in step 2 and use 3tbsp of water instead of orange juice to make the icing in step 6.

Ingredients for 20-24 biscuits

125g (4oz) self-raising flour

60g (2oz) unsalted butter (diced) + extra for greasing

60g (2oz) soft dark brown sugar

½ egg yolk (beaten)

1tbsp of clear runny honey

1tsp of orange zest

For the icing

225g (7½oz) icing sugar (sieved)

3tbsp of fresh orange juice

1. Preheat the oven to 180°C (350°F/Gas 4). **Sieve** the flour into a bowl and **rub** the butter into the flour, until you have a breadcrumb texture.

2. Using a table knife, stir the sugar, orange zest, honey, and egg into the flour and butter, until the mixture starts to come together in lumps.

Chef's tip
When slicing the dough in step 5, turn the log 90° after each slice to produce evenly-shaped biscuits. If the dough breaks, you can just re-shape it.

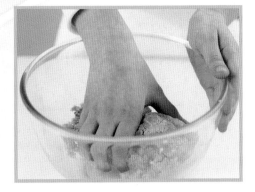

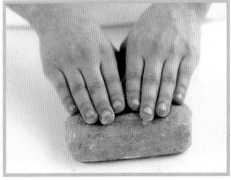

3. Use your hands to bring the lumps together to form a ball of dough. Briefly **knead** the dough and then lightly flour the work surface.

4. Roll the dough into a log, about 5cm (2") in diameter and 10cm (4") long. Wrap the log in cling film and chill it for 1½ hours, or until firm.

5. Lightly grease the baking sheets with butter. **Slice** the log into 20–24 thin discs and place the biscuits on the baking sheets. Bake for 7–9 minutes.

6. Remove the biscuits from the oven, allow them to set, and put them on a rack to cool. **Beat** the icing sugar and orange juice until they form a smooth paste.

7. Carefully transfer the biscuits to a cooling rack. Put the icing into a piping bag and then **drizzle** it over the cool biscuits in your favourite patterns.

● **preparation** 1 hour 15 minutes ● **chilling** 1 hour 15 minutes ● **cooking** 1 hour 5 minutes

Vegetable tart

This is a simple introduction to making savoury shortcrust pastry. Here's a top tip – when making savoury or sweet pastry, make sure that your hands are not too hot and the butter and water are also cool to give the pastry a lighter texture.

The technique used in step 6 is called baking blind.

Tools

- ☐ sieve
- ☐ mixing bowl
- ☐ fork
- ☐ tablespoon
- ☐ cling film
- ☐ rolling pin
- ☐ flan tin, loose-bottomed and fluted (approx. 20cm/8" in diameter)
- ☐ table knife
- ☐ greaseproof paper
- ☐ baking beans or dried kidney beans
- ☐ oven gloves
- ☐ jug
- ☐ whisk

Recipe idea
Other fillings, such as bacon, peppers, broccoli, onion, or mushrooms would taste great in this recipe.

Ingredients for 1 tart

225g (7½oz) plain flour + extra for rolling

1 pinch of salt

2 tbsp of water

90g (3oz) unsalted butter (diced)

30g (1oz) vegetable fat or lard (cubed)

For the filling

2 eggs (beaten)

100ml (3½ fl oz) cream

125g (4oz) peas

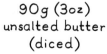
30g (1oz) cheese (grated)

100g (3½oz) ham (cubed)

1 small leek (sautéed)

125g (4oz) sweetcorn

100ml (3½ fl oz) milk

1. **Sieve** the flour and salt into a bowl. Using a fork, gently stir the diced butter and vegetable fat into the flour until they are completely coated.

2. **Rub** the butter and fat into the flour with your fingertips, until it looks like coarse breadcrumbs. Preheat the oven to 200°C (400°F/Gas 6).

3. Add the water, drop by drop, and stir it into the crumbs with a table knife. When the crumbs start to stick together in lumps, gather the pastry in your hands.

4. Shape the pastry into a smooth disc and wrap it in cling film. Chill it for 1 hour, or until firm. Lightly flour the work surface.

Serving tip
Sprinkle the cheese over the top and bake the tart for 45 minutes. Allow the tart to set and cool before serving.

5. **Roll** out the pastry so that it is slightly bigger than the tin. Gently press it into the tin and trim off the excess. Prick the base and chill it for 15 minutes.

6. Cover the tart with 2 layers of greaseproof paper and add the baking beans. Bake for 15 minutes, remove the paper and beans and bake for 5 minutes.

7. Reduce the oven to 180°C (350°F/Gas 4). Scatter the ham and vegetables over the base. **Whisk** the eggs, milk, and cream together and pour into the tart.

Apple pie

When making a sweet or savoury pie, it is important to make a hole in the top of the pastry, before you bake it. This allows the steam to escape and stops the pastry going soggy! Making sweet pastry is very similar to savoury pastry so read the recipe carefully to note the important differences!

Tools

☐ sieve

☐ 2 large mixing bowls

☐ fork

☐ table knife

☐ cling film

☐ wooden spoon

☐ pie dish (approx 22cm /8½" in diameter)

☐ rolling pin

☐ pastry brush

☐ oven gloves

Recipe idea
Make sure that you use apples that are suitable for cooking and eating, such as Cox's, Golden Delicious, or Mcintosh.

The fruit from the crumble on p.90-91 would taste great in this recipe.

Ingredients for 1 pie

225g (7½oz) plain flour

1 pinch of salt

125g (4oz) unsalted butter (diced)

1 egg yolk (beaten with 15ml/1tbsp water)

2tbsp of caster sugar

1 egg beaten (for glazing)

For the filling

750g (1½lb) apples (peeled, cored, and cut into wedges)

1tsp of vanilla extract

½ tsp of ground cinnamon

60g (2oz) soft light brown sugar

½ orange (zest and juice)

60g (2oz) chopped walnuts (optional)

1. Sieve the flour and salt into the bowl and stir in the sugar. Using a fork, gently stir the diced butter into the flour until it is completely coated.

2. Using your fingertips, **rub** the diced butter into the flour. When the butter is fully mixed in, the mixture will look like coarse breadcrumbs.

3. Stir the water and egg yolk (drop by drop) into the crumbs with a table knife until they stick together in lumps. Gather the pastry in your hands.

4. Put the pastry onto a lightly-floured work surface and shape it into a smooth disc. Wrap the disc in cling film and chill it for 1 hour, or until firm.

Chef's tip
Use the excess pastry from step 6 to make leaf shapes and decorate the pie. Put them on top of the pie before baking in step 7.

5. Preheat the oven to 220°C (425°F/Gas 7). Mix the sugar, cinnamon, vanilla extract, orange juice, zest, walnuts, and apples together in a bowl.

6. Tip the filling into the dish. Dampen the edge of the dish. **Roll** the pastry out to about 3mm (⅛") thick and place it over the dish. Trim the excess.

7. Press the edges of the pastry into the dish and **crimp** with a fork. **Glaze** the pie with egg and make a hole in the centre. Bake for 30–35 minutes, until golden.

● preparation 35-40 minutes   ● cooking 25-30 minutes

Chocolate cake

When baking a cake make sure that the oven is at the right temperature before you put the cake in. When the cake is in the oven, don't open the door to check on it until the cooking time has passed, otherwise it will sink!

Tools

- ☐ 2 round cake tins, non stick (approx 20cm/8" in diameter)
- ☐ baking parchment
- ☐ large mixing bowl
- ☐ electric whisk
- ☐ sieve
- ☐ metal mixing spoon
- ☐ step palette knife
- ☐ oven gloves
- ☐ cooling rack
- ☐ small mixing bowl
- ☐ small saucepan
- ☐ rubber spoon spatula
- ☐ serving plate

For a flat top, put the second cake on upside down!

Recipe idea
For a tasty topping, melt 100g (3½ oz) white chocolate (see step 4) and pour it into a wax paper-lined tray. Leave it to set. Break the set chocolate into small pieces and use it to decorate the top of the cake.

Ingredients for 1 cake

3 beaten eggs (at room temperature)

175g (6oz) unsalted butter (softened)

175g (6oz) caster sugar

½ tsp of baking powder

oil (for greasing)

150g (5oz) self raising flour

3tbsp of cocoa powder

For the topping

100g (3½oz) milk chocolate

200ml (7fl oz) double cream (at room temperature)

100g (3½oz) plain chocolate

1. **Grease** the cake tins and **line** the bases. **Cream** the butter and sugar together in a bowl until they are light and fluffy. Gradually **beat** in the egg.

2. Preheat the oven to 180°C (350°F/Gas 4). **Sieve** the flour, cocoa powder, and baking powder into the bowl and **fold** them into the creamed mixture.

Food fact
The beaten eggs used in step 1 should be at room temperature and added slowly, otherwise the cake mixture may curdle. If the mixture does start to curdle, mix in a little flour.

3. Divide the mixture equally between the two greased and lined cake tins, smoothing the tops with a palette knife. Bake for 20–25 minutes or until firm.

4. Turn the cooked cakes out onto a cooling rack. Break the plain and milk chocolate into a bowl and gently **melt** them over a pan of simmering water.

5. Remove the bowl from the pan. Allow the chocolate to cool for 5 minutes and then stir in the cream. Leave the mixture to thicken for a few minutes.

6. Make sure the cakes are completely cool before putting on the topping. Put one cake on a serving plate and spread a quarter of the topping over it.

7. Put the other cake on top and spoon over the rest of the topping. Spread it over the top and the sides until the cake is evenly coated. Leave to set.

Tools

Here is a handy guide to all the equipment used in this book.
Each recipe has a tools checklist so that you can gather
everything you need before you begin cooking:

The basic tools

oven gloves

tin opener

colander

toaster

tablespoon

teaspoon

dessert spoon

fork

mixing bowl

knife

Baking tools

(non-stick) baking sheet

baking tray

(non-stick) baking tray

rectangular cake tin

cooling rack

loose-bottomed, fluted flan tin

(non-stick) loaf tin

roasting tin

round cake tin

square cake tin

rolling pin

sieve

cookie cutter

(non-stick) muffin tray

step palette knife

cake slice

pastry brush

paper muffin case

Crushing, juicing and blending

blender

food processor

hand blender

garlic crusher

masher

reamer (for juicing)

Cutting and chopping

bread knife

carving knife

cook's knife

vegetable peeler

scissors

chopping board

grater

paring knife

utility knife

Spoons and spatulas

ladle

plastic spatula

rubber spoon spatula

slotted metal spoon

slotted wooden spatula

wooden spatula

wooden spoon

metal spatula

pasta spoon

metal mixing and serving spoon

tongs

Whisking

flat whisk

electric whisk

balloon whisk

Measuring and weighing

measuring spoons

scales

measuring jug

Pots and pans

saucepan

frying pan

wok

sauté pan

griddle pan

Miscellaneous tools

pie dish

small ovenproof dish

ovenproof dish

wooden kebab skewers

lolly mould and sticks

bamboo rolling mat

Glossary

This is the place to find extra information about the cookery words and techniques used in this book. Key terms are explained simply, plus there are chef's tips to give you even more handy hints.

Cutting words

Food is often cut into smaller pieces to make it easier to cook with and eat. Here are some cutting words:

Chopping – cutting into smaller pieces with a knife.
Coring – removing the core of a fruit. The core is the hard central part of some fruit, such as apples.
Crushing – breaking food up into very small pieces e.g. with a garlic crusher.
Cubing – cutting food into cubes about 2.5cm (1").
De-seeding – removing the seeds of fruit and vegetables, such as peppers, tomatoes, and cucumber.
Dicing – cutting into small cubes.
Grating – rubbing food against a grater to make coarse or fine shreds.
Hulling – cutting off the green stalks and leaves of fruit, such as strawberries.
Juicing – squeezing the liquid from fruit or vegetables.
Mashing – crushing food, such as bananas or cooked potatoes, to make a smooth mass.
Peeling – removing the skin or outer layer of vegetables and fruit, by hand or with a knife. Some vegetables, such as onions and garlic, are always peeled first.
Roughly chopping – cutting into pieces of varying sizes.
Scoring – making long, shallow cuts in food, to reduce cooking time or allow flavour to be absorbed.
Slicing – cutting food into thick or thin pieces.
Stoning – removing the large stone at the centre of some fruit, such as peaches or mangoes.
Strips – long, thick or thin pieces.
Tailing – removing the stalk of a vegetable.
Trimming – cutting off the unwanted parts (such as roots or leaves) of fruit, vegetables, meat, or fish.
Zesting – finely grating the peel of oranges, lemons, or limes to make zest, which is used as a flavouring.

★ Chef's tips

How to dice an onion

First cut the onion in half through the root and then peel off the skin. Place one half flat-side-down and firmly hold the onion so that the root is near your little finger. Carefully cut parallel slices, horizontally towards the root (step 1). Turn the root of the onion away from you and slice, downwards from the root (Step 2). Turn the root back towards your little finger and slice across so that the onion falls away in small cubes (Step 3). To chop an onion, just follow steps 2 and 3.

Step 1

Step 2

Step 3

How to crush garlic

crushing garlic

Break open the garlic bulb and remove the cloves. Peel each clove and place them in a garlic crusher, one at a time. Squeeze the handle to crush the garlic and press it through the holes.

How to de-seed a pepper

Cut the top off the pepper. Inside you will see the core and the seeds. Carefully cut any parts attached to the side of the pepper and pull out the core and seeds.

de-seeding

How to juice an orange

juicing

Cut an orange in half. Hold each half in turn over a bowl and press a reamer or juicer into the centre. Twist the orange or reamer so that the juice drips into the bowl and then remove any pips.

Cooking words

Many of the recipes ask you to **preheat** the oven or grill, which means to heat it to the correct temperature before you begin. This helps the food to cook thoroughly and evenly. Here are some other words to help you:

Baking – cooking food in an oven with dry heat (without any liquid). The outside will become brown.
Basting – spooning hot fat or a marinade during cooking to prevent drying out.
Boiling – when a liquid, such as water reaches boiling point it bubbles and is very hot.
Dry-frying – frying without oil or fat.
Frying – cooking in a frying pan or saucepan with a little oil, over direct heat.
Griddling – cooking or browning in a griddle pan, on a hob.
Grilling – cooking or browning under intense heat.
Par-boiling – boiling for half the normal cooking time to soften, not completely cook.
Poaching – cooking in gently simmering liquid.
Reducing – simmering a liquid, such as a sauce, so that it thickens and reduces in quantity.
Roasting – cooking in the oven at a high temperature.
Sautéing – frying quickly in a little oil or fat.
Shallow-frying – frying in about 1.25cm (½") or more of oil so that the food becomes golden and crispy.
Simmering – cooking over a low heat so the liquid or food is bubbling gently but not boiling.
Stir-frying – frying quickly in a little oil or fat over a high heat, stirring constantly.
Toasting – browning and crisping food under a grill, in a toaster, or in the oven.
Warming – heating gently over a low heat, without boiling.

★ Chef's tips

How to roast a red pepper
Pre-heat the oven to 220°C (425°F/Gas 7). Brush a pepper with oil and place it on a roasting tin. Roast for 30 minutes or until the skin starts to blacken. Allow the pepper to cool before peeling and de-seeding.

How to check that meat is cooked
It is really important that you always check that meat is cooked thoroughly. Although meat sometimes looks cooked on the outside, you should check that the centre is not pink or bloody. To check a roast chicken, stick a skewer into the centre or thickest part of the meat. If the juices that run out are clear (not bloody or pink), then the meat is thoroughly cooked.

roast chicken

Mixing words

Mixing means to combine ingredients together. There are lots of mixing words.

Beating – stirring or mixing quickly until smooth, to break down or add air.
Blending – mixing ingredients together using a blender or food processor, to form a liquid or smooth mass.
Creaming – beating butter and sugar together to incorporate air.
Folding – a gentle way of mixing ingredients together, to retain as much air in the mixture as possible.
Whipping – beating ingredients, such as cream or egg whites, to add air and make them thicker.
Whisking – evenly mixing ingredients, with a whisk; another word for whipping.

★ Chef's tips

How to beat an egg
To beat an egg, crack the egg into a bowl and stir vigorously with a fork or whisk.

beating

How to cream butter and sugar
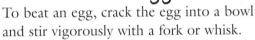
Dice the butter and then allow it to soften a little. Whisk the butter and sugar together or beat them with a wooden spoon to incorporate air and make a light and fluffy mixture.

creaming

How to fold ingredients
Use a metal spoon or rubber spatula to gently lift and turn the ingredients until they are just about mixed together, to avoid losing precious air in the mixture.

folding

How to whip cream

Use a hand or electric whisk to vigorously whip the cream until it forms soft, firm peaks. Do not over-whip as this will make the cream curdle.

whipping

Bread-making

Bread-making is a lot of fun but you'll need a lot of energy for all that kneading! Here are some useful bread-making terms:

Kneading – pressing and folding the dough with your hands until it is smooth and stretchy. This distributes the yeast and helps it to rise.

Knocking back – deflating the dough with a gentle punch. This evens out the texture of the bread.

Proving – this is the correct name for the process of rising in bread-making.

Rising – the time it takes for the dough to increase in size.

★ Chef's tips

How to knead dough

kneading

Lightly sprinkle flour on the work surface and use one hand to hold the dough. With the heel of the other hand, gently push the dough away from you and then lift the dough back over. Repeat for about 10 minutes until the dough is smooth and stretchy, rotating frequently for even kneading.

How to knock back dough

knocking back

After the dough has risen and doubled in size, it will need to be knocked back. Press down firmly with your knuckles and the dough will deflate.

- -

Pastry-making

Shortcrust pastry is the type usually used for pies or tarts. **Puff** pastry is light and flaky. Here are some useful pastry words:

Baking blind – weighing down pastry with baking beans to stop it rising or changing shape during baking.

Crimping – sealing or decorating the edges of pastry with a fork or by pinching with your fingers.

Glazing – brushing egg yolk or milk on to pastry (or dough) to make it look shiny when cooked.

Rolling – flattening the pastry with a rolling pin to make a bigger, thinner sheet.

Rubbing – mixing fat into the flour with your fingertips until it resembles breadcrumbs.

★ Chef's tips

How to roll pastry or dough

rolling pastry

Sprinkle some flour onto the work surface and rolling pin. Roll the rolling pin across the pastry, away from you. Rotate the pastry and sprinkle more flour, if needed. Keep rolling and rotating until you get the right shape and thickness. Always roll the pastry slightly bigger than you need.

How to bake blind

baking blind

Cover the pastry with a double layer of greaseproof paper and weigh it down with baking beans or dried beans. Bake blind for 15 minutes, or as directed in the recipe and then remove the paper and beans.

- -

Cake-making

Here are some useful cake-making words:

Greasing – lightly coating the inside of a cake tin or other surface with oil or fat to prevent sticking.

Lining – covering the insides of a cake tin with parchment paper to prevent sticking.

Melting – heating a solid, such as chocolate or butter, to turn it into a liquid.

Sieving – to put a powdery ingredient, such as flour, through a sieve to remove lumps and aerate the mixture.

★ Chef's tips

How to grease and line a cake tin

lining

greasing

With a pencil, draw around the cake tin onto some parchment or greaseproof paper. Cut around the outline with scissors. Grease the tin by rubbing butter or oil all over the inside, using a small piece of parchment paper. Lay the paper on the bottom of the tin.

How to test that a cake is cooked

testing a cake

Insert a skewer or knife into the centre of a cake. If it comes out clean (without any cake mixture) the cake is cooked. If the skewer comes out with mixture on it, bake for a few more minutes.

Egg words

All the recipes in this book use medium-sized eggs, which should be at room temperature. The names for the parts of an egg are:

Shell – the hard outer covering of the egg.
White – the clear, runny part of the egg that turns white when cooked.
Yolk – the yellow ball in the centre of the egg.

★ Chef's tips

How to check for freshness

fresh egg test

Most eggs have a "use-by" date on them but here is a handy tip: place an egg in a glass of water – if it is fresh (good), the egg will lie horizontally on the bottom, but if it is stale (bad), it will stand upright and pop up to the top of the glass. You should never use a stale egg.

cracking an egg

How to crack an egg

Tap the egg firmly on the side of a bowl or jug, gently pull the sides apart, and let the insides drop into the container. It is best to crack an egg into a separate dish before adding it to your mixture, in case bits of the shell fall in as well!

How to separate an egg

Crack the egg over a bowl and break it open gently. Don't let the yolk fall into the bowl – tip it carefully from one half of the shell to the other until all the white has dropped into the bowl. Put the yolk into a separate bowl.

separating an egg white from the yolk

Useful words

Here are some more words that you will learn in this book:

Absorb – to soak up, usually during cooking.
Batter – a runny mixture made of flour, eggs, and milk.
Caramelizing – turning brown and sticky when heated; this happens if the food has a sweet coating or sauce.
Chill – to cool in a refrigerator.

Coat – to cover with a layer of something, such as flour.
Curdle – when the liquid and solid parts of an ingredient or mixture separate. Milk curdles when over-heated and cakes curdle if the eggs are too cold or added too quickly.
Dash – a small quantity.
Defrost – to thaw frozen food.
Dollop – a large spoonful of a soft food.
Drain – to remove unwanted liquid, sometimes with a colander or sieve.
Drizzle – to pour slowly, in a trickle.
Drop – a single splash of liquid.
Freeze – to turn a liquid into a solid by storing it in an extremely cold place (freezer).
Knob – a small lump of a solid ingredient, such as butter.
Marinade – a mixture of oil, herbs, spices, and other flavourings in which food is soaked to add flavour.
Marinate – to soak meat, fish, or vegetables in a marinade in order to add flavour or tenderize.
Paste – a soft, thick mixture.
Pinch – as much of a powdery ingredient as you can hold between your finger and thumb.
Prick – to make small air holes, usually with a fork.
Purée – a thick pulp produced by blending or sieving.
Refresh – to rinse a just-cooked food, such as pasta, in cold water to prevent further cooking.
Rest – to set aside cooked food for a short time, such as roasted meat, to allow it to become tender and moist.
Rinse – to wash in running water from the tap.
Ripe – when a fruit is soft and ready to be eaten.
Scatter – to roughly sprinkle pieces of an ingredient or food over something with your hands.
Seal – to join up or encase a food to prevent anything getting in or out.
Season – to add salt and pepper to a food to balance and enhance its natural flavour.
Set – to turn from a liquid into a solid.
Shape – to use your hands to turn a soft food or mixture into a particular shape.
Sieve – to use a sieve to drain liquid, remove lumps, or add air.
Sprinkle – to scatter a food lightly over something.
Stand – to set a food aside for a while to cool, finish cooking, or improve the flavour.
Stock – a flavoured liquid in which meat, fish, or vegetables are cooked.
Thicken – to add an ingredient, such as flour, to make a liquid less thin.
Wedges – thick slices with a pointed or thin edge.

Index